Teaching AIDS

T0386590

Douglas Tonks

Teaching AIDS

Routledge ▪ New York
and
London

Published 1996 by Routledge

711 Third Avenue
New York, NY, 10017

2 Park Square
Milton Park, Abingdon, Oxon, OX14 4RN

Copyright © 1996 by Routledge

Routledge is an imprint of the Taylor & Francis Group, an informa business

Library of Congress Cataloging–in–Publication Data
Tonks, Douglas.
     Teaching AIDS / by Douglas Tonks.
          p.   cm.
     Includes bibliographical references and index.
     ISBN 0–415–90874–4. —ISBN 0–415–90875–2 (pbk.)
     1. AIDS (Disease)—Study and teaching. 2. AIDS (Disease)—
Prevention. I. Title.
RA644.A25T635   1995   95-30105
616.97'9205—dc20   CIP

British Library Cataloging–in–Publication Data also available

Contents

         Appropriate Age to Begin AIDS Instruction ■ Young
         Children ■ Older Children ■ Teenagers

5   Individual and Group Activities to Uncover the Facts   69
         Getting Things Started ■ Multi Media ■ Group Activ-
         ities ■ Solitary Activities ■ Lecture and Information
         Delivery ■ Conclusion

6   Skills to Change Student Attitudes Toward AIDS and Risky
         Behavior   99
         Affecting Behavior Through Attitude ■ Refusal Skills

7   Modeling the Skills   125
         Modifying Modeling for Your Classroom ■ Modeling
         an AIDS-Specific Scenario

8   Skill-Building Classroom Activities   151
         Role-Playing ■ Peer Education ■ Drama

         Notes   167
         Bibliography   173
         Index   191

Preface

In his monologue, *Gray's Anatomy*, Spalding Gray is faced with deteriorating eyesight and potential blindness. He describes his initial reaction to the problem: "It was so terrifying that I had no choice but to ignore it." Since it first came to attention in the early 1980s, acquired immunodeficiency syndrome (AIDS) has inspired much the same response. Although the disease has disrupted a generation with its deadly presence, become the leading cause of death for young adults in the United States, and pervaded our culture in any number of ways, the level of ignorance, misinformation, and disinterest we still hold about the human immunodeficiency virus (HIV) and the disease it leads to is astonishing.

So far the medical community has had little luck in combating and understanding HIV. Instead of responsibly confronting the virus, many in the public sector have ignored it. Paul Monette writes, "It will be recorded that the dead in the first decade of the calamity died of our indifference." [1] Perhaps the specter of inevitable death and debilitation that seems to hover around the disease has made it too frightening for us to face as a society. Despite our best intentions, we cannot confront AIDS directly.

For whatever reason, we have left the most vulnerable part of our society, our children and adolescents, to fend for themselves without the protection of knowledge and information, dying of our indifference. The future seems to hold no concerted educational effort to shield them from the human immunodeficiency virus. This book is an attempt to remedy that by giving teachers the tools they need to institute an AIDS educational program themselves. With the information and techniques provided here, individual teachers will have the ability to give their students a background of knowledge that can save their lives from the ravages of this disease.

Acknowledgments

This book would not have been completed without the invaluable help of some important people. I thank Frank Peppiatt for kindly providing his support during the process of its writing. Betsy Hall offered insightful advice and suggestions in reading the manuscript. Frank Fredrickson and Debbie Chilco were helpful in locating and securing sources. My thanks also go to Eva Burgess for allowing me to observe her at work, and to Wendy Arnold and all at Peer Education Project/Los Angeles. To Spalding Gray for providing the quotation from his work, and to Bruce Gilray who, in addition to offering assistance on this project, demonstrated how to respond to this disease before finally being defeated by it in 1995. I thank my father for his promotional ideas and my mother for helping me realize when the book was finished. Sarah Linn deserves mention for all her bibliographic help. And finally, I must thank my wife Francesca for her support and advice throughout the life of this project.

Teaching AIDS

The Extent of the Problem of AIDS and HIV in Adolescents

Adolescent AIDS has been the subject of relatively little attention since the AIDS pandemic began. The majority of concern has been given to the more obvious presence of adult cases of AIDS and their implications. Perhaps this is as it should be; AIDS first came to our attention among adults, and the bulk of AIDS cases appear in adults. After adults, AIDS cases among children have received the most attention. AIDS babies born to HIV-positive mothers or infected by the virus in their mother's milk are the embodiment of the innocent "victim" of the AIDS crisis. Helpless to aid themselves, they deserve and receive the sympathy of the world. Caught between the overwhelming manifestation of AIDS in adults and the compassionate portrayal of infants with AIDS are a vast number of adolescents at risk of HIV infection whose peril has been largely ignored by the media and by their parents and teachers. Grouped with either adults or children, or sometimes not present in the equation at all, the needs and responses specific to youths have fallen through the cracks of AIDS prevention and care.

Part of the reason that the effects of AIDS in adolescents have been relatively easy to set aside is that the number of reports of actual AIDS cases among teenagers has been quite small. Few teenagers have AIDS, for some very understandable reasons. Babies infected with HIV rarely survive into their teen years. On the other hand, adolescents who come into contact with HIV will likely not become symptomatic and be diagnosed with AIDS until they have entered their twenties. Just because there is not an overwhelming incidence of AIDS among teenagers, however, does not mean that many are not infected. In fact, researchers fear that HIV infection among this group has been drastically underestimated and that the actual number of HIV-positive teens doubles every year.[1]

To see that AIDS is a problem among teens, we can take the number of AIDS cases or HIV infections currently present in young adults to identify how many teenagers were infected over the past decade. Dr. Michael Merson, Director General of the World Health Organization Global Programme on AIDS, estimates that half of worldwide HIV infections since the beginning of the pandemic occurred among fifteen- to twenty-four-year-olds.[2]

We must assume that HIV is currently active among the students in our junior high and high schools. Even if the incidence of AIDS itself never becomes a pressing issue in the schools, HIV is already there, and we must assume it is spreading. Dr. Karen Hein, the director of the Adolescent AIDS Program at the Montfiore Medical Center in the Bronx, and perhaps the leading advocate for studying the problem of AIDS among adolescents, suggests that only two factors are necessary for the rapid spread of HIV among teenagers: "unprotected sexual intercourse and the presence of the virus."[3] HIV, although hidden, is present among teenagers; unfortunately, so is Hein's first factor, unprotected sexual intercourse.

TEENAGE SEXUAL ACTIVITY

Although adults often refuse to recognize or believe the facts of teenage sexuality, these realities are very difficult to deny. Societies throughout history have generally been unwilling to admit it, but some teenagers have always been active in exploring their sexual identities and abilities. It is a part of growing up. Whether or not she was sexually active may be a matter of interpretation, but Juliet was only thirteen when she began her star-crossed romance with

Romeo, himself only a year or two older. The level of passion they shared remains a part of the adolescent experience. In the past generation, teenage sexual activity has increased. Recent surveys have revealed that three-quarters or more of all teenagers, male and female, have had sexual intercourse before their twentieth birthday.[4]

Making these numbers somewhat menacing is the fact that much of this sexual activity is risky in one form or another. For the most part, sexually active teenagers are not monogamous. The ages between fifteen and nineteen are the most likely ages for individuals to experiment with multiple partners. A simple exploration of high school romances can confirm this fact. Many teens juggle more than one partner of the opposite sex simultaneously, and even those who remain monogamous do so for a very short time. Teenage romances often last only a few weeks, the long-term couples staying together a mere matter of months, creating a pattern of serial monogamy. A teenager may be faithful to one partner at a time, but over the period of his or her teen years, several partners are likely to have come and gone. Further, when sex is practiced by adolescent couples, the use of condoms or any other sort of contraception is very low. Often up to a year can pass between a teenager's first sexual experience and his or her reliable use of contraception. While various types of contraception can protect against unintended pregnancy, only condoms provide protection against HIV and other sexually transmitted diseases as well. As proof of these trends, we need look no farther than the one million teenage pregnancies and two-and-a-half million cases of sexually transmitted disease (STD) that occur among teenagers every year.[5]

Sexually Transmitted Diseases

It is in examining sexually transmitted diseases that the closest analogy to HIV and AIDS can be made. STDs, such as gonorrhea, herpes, and syphilis, are diseases that are transmitted from person to person, as their name implies, through sexual activity. Keeping track of these diseases provides researchers with one method of measuring sexual activity. Two-and-a-half million cases of STDs among teenagers each year sounds imposing enough; when taken as a percentage of sexually active adolescents, rather than the overall teenage population, STD rates are the highest of any age group—double that of adults in their twenties. Cumulatively, the proportion of teens who have ever been infected with an STD, not just within the last year, is estimated by the U.S. Department of Health and Human Services to be twenty-five percent.[6] AIDS follows a similar pattern.

Although adolescents are infected as a result of homosexual sexual activity and intravenous drug use, the presence of heterosexual transmission is higher than among the general population. Forty-one percent of adolescent women with AIDS were infected as a result of heterosexual contact.[7]

Adolescent AIDS Knowledge

Unfortunately, adolescent risk activity is not due to a lack of knowledge concerning HIV and AIDS. There is little doubt that the majority of teenagers have mastered basic AIDS information. They can tell you that there is no cure, that HIV infection more often than not leads to death, that the virus spreads through blood and sexual fluids, and which activities are likely to put them at risk. Most teens are aware of all this, yet they continue to engage in activities putting them at risk. Simple knowledge is not enough to change risky behavior. In virtually every documented case, adolescents have practiced the same level of risk behavior after learning the facts about AIDS as before.[8] Information is not enough to bring about any meaningful change in behavior. In fact, in what may be a precursor to attitudes among teenagers in the near future, a new generation of young gay men is returning to the high-risk sex of the pre-AIDS era. Older gays saw their community decimated by the disease, and learned to practice safer sex to protect themselves. Younger gays, perhaps envious of the apparent freedom practiced by their predecessors, have begun to live their sex lives as if AIDS had never existed, engaging in unprotected intercourse with multiple partners.[9] If teenagers follow this example, jealous of the sexual liberties taken by the generation preceding them and determined to seize those sexual liberties for themselves, they will usher in a new wave of HIV exposure and AIDS devastation.

ADOLESCENT ATTITUDES TOWARD SEXUALITY

Teenagers hold a peculiar place in our society. They are taking their first few steps into adulthood, but are not yet free of all the restrictions of childhood. They are changing both psychologically and physiologically, but are discouraged from acting out or exploring many of these changes. Because most teenagers remain under their parents' wing, their experiments with independence must be carried out either within the confines of parental control or without their parents finding out.

Sexual activity is one of the basic areas in which adolescents begin to exert their independence. In many ways, teens feel that sexual exploration is expected of them. Our society recognizes sexual activity as a normal behavior among adults, and teens merely want to join in, to assume the mantle of maturity sex appears to bring with it. Instead of providing socially acceptable routes of sexual expression for young people, society instead contributes convoluted and confusing messages through movies, television, and advertising that characterize sex as extremely enticing but denied to young people. As childhood turns into adolescence, youths experience new sexual appetites that demand some sort of reaction. In the absence of socially approved methods of sexual exploration, teenagers will investigate their newfound interests on their own. In the process, their sexual activity provides an enticing avenue through which they can forge their independence and join the adult world.

Sexual activity, particularly under the specter of AIDS, also allows the opportunity for that time-tested adolescent activity, teenage rebellion. To some degree, it may not really matter what rules adults set down about sex or what attitudes they hold on the subject. Some teenagers will act against what they perceive the attitudes of adults to be, no matter what the reality is. Adults, and particularly parents, stereotypically hold the view that adolescents should stay away from any and all sexual activity, and this in and of itself may be enough to encourage many teenagers to begin their experimentation.

On top of this desire to experiment, many teens may also hold a degree of anger over the intrusion of AIDS into their reality. They are warned to abstain from sex, or at the very least to practice "safe sex," by the very people whose generation initiated the "sexual revolution." Instead of studying the facts about AIDS, too many adolescents, intent on carrying out their own personal sexual revolution, ignore the message of parents whom they see as recent converts to a new moral standard that they themselves previously threw off. In fact, too many teens take the attitude that AIDS is one more barrier to their sexual liberty. "If you won't abstain because of morality," they imagine adults to be thinking, "we'll threaten you with death."

Communication between parents and adolescents on any subject has never been strong, and the record is even more dismal on the subject of sex. Parents tend to shy away from raising the subject with their children at any age, and thus lose their authority to present either information or their own attitudes on the subject. Some research suggests that parental communication, when it does take place, has very little effect, positive or negative, on sexual behavior. Instead, friends fill the vacuum.[10] Adolescents, by and large, turn their backs on all adults, from parents and teachers to scientists and public health experts, when it comes to this subject. The adult agenda on sex seems clear to them: "Just Say No." Teenagers take their defiant attitude even farther in dealing with AIDS, tending to be skeptical about basic AIDS facts and trusting no information from any source.[11] In fact, AIDS education may even suffer a backlash from teens, just as anti-drug efforts did in the sixties, if the message seems to overstate the actual facts of HIV and AIDS in an attempt to frighten teens into adopting safe behaviors. An initial thrust of AIDS educators must be to reinforce and, if necessary, regain the trust of teens. The only influence parents can wield to delay their children's sexual initiation is through their teaching of values. When teenagers share their parents' values and feel close ties within their family, they tend to wait longer before taking part in sexual intercourse.[12]

Risk-Taking

Of course, simple defiance is not the only reason for adolescents to experiment with their sexuality. Adolescence is a time of testing boundaries, of questioning previously held ideas, of probing oneself, and of trying new things. One of the hallmarks of adolescence is taking risks. Teenagers do not limit their risk-taking simply to sex. One way to gauge the extent of teen risk-taking is to examine the risks that do not work out, such as accidents. Teens have a higher rate of all forms of accidents than do adults, particularly automobile accidents. This adolescent risk-taking also extends to risks with their health, of which unsafe sex is only a part.

The psychology of adolescent risk-taking is not completely understood, but one apparent factor is the assumption of teenage invulnerability. This term is misunderstood by many people who insist that teenagers do not consciously think that they can withstand any threat, that they are impervious to harm. Of course teenagers are not foolish enough to imagine that bullets will bounce off them or that they will walk away unhurt from a smashed car. Teenagers do not believe they *can*not be harmed, they believe that they *will* not be harmed. Adolescents can take risks with unsafe sex because they do not suppose they will ever come into contact with someone infected with HIV.

It is far too easy for teenagers, as well as many adults, to see AIDS as someone else's disease. When AIDS first came to national attention, it was portrayed primarily as a disease of gay men and IV drug users. Health experts have always maintained that HIV would make its way into the mainstream heterosexual community, but that initial image of HIV risk groups has held steady. Sexually active heterosexual adolescents look at themselves and see that they and their partners are not gay men and do not take IV drugs. Based on such reasoning, they assume that they do not need to worry about becoming infected with HIV. Even those to whom the idea of becoming infected does occur dismiss it out of hand as an insubstantial risk.

Fear and Denial

Another element that will influence adolescent response to the threat of HIV and AIDS is fear. A modicum of fear might be helpful in persuading teenagers to protect themselves from the virus, but too much fear can backfire. Fear can spawn different types of reactions, primary among them regression and denial. Faced with overwhelming fear, teens might regress to depression and a state of dependence. Denial, however, is an entirely different matter. Instead of the fatalistic assumption that a teen has probably already been infected with HIV and has nothing else to lose, denial will not allow a teen to examine the problem at all. Denial is a very dangerous state for a teenager to reach, because any information that contradicts the assumption of denial will be immediately dismissed. Instead of facing up to the horror of a terrible, life-ending disease, teenagers find it much easier to pretend that this disease does not happen to people like them.

Making the reality of AIDS even easier for teens to deny are the very characteristics of the infection itself. HIV infection can remain asymptomatic for more than ten years. Because asymptomatic HIV-positive individuals show no apparent sickness, it is virtually inconceivable to most youth that these individuals can be carrying a fatal virus. Much of our society remains in denial over the issue of AIDS, so one can hardly be surprised when teenagers follow suit. But the effects of denial should not be underestimated. Denial has been shown to be so extreme in some cases that pregnant teenage girls will deny the fact of their pregnancy until they enter labor.[13]

Recent surveys that reveal the numbers of teens who overstate their own risk of becoming infected with HIV have illustrated the seeds of the overwhelming fear that can lead to denial among adolescents. One study found that seventy-five percent of those questioned feared getting AIDS. Students in another poll greatly exaggerated the risk of infection from one act of unprotected sex.[14] While the risk to these adolescents is present and must be addressed, it is not as high as they believe. Such overstatements of risk can lead adolescents to feel overwhelmed with the entire issue of AIDS, and set the stage for massive denial.

Self-Esteem and Peer Pressure

Adolescent decision-making is also dependent on two factors that circle back and forth and around each other: self-esteem and peer pressure. Teenagers' ability to resist the pressure exerted on them by their peers hinges on the strength of their self-esteem, which, in turn, is influenced to some extent by those same peers. But self-esteem is affected by other considerations as well. As mentioned earlier, parents can still influence their adolescent children through the values that they have instilled in them throughout their lives. Adolescents with deeply held religious beliefs and practices appear in general to have higher self-esteem and tend to enter into sexual activity at a later time than adolescents who do not. Self-esteem is also tied into academic performance. High academic achievers appear to have higher self-esteem than do low achievers. When low- achieving students come to the conclusion that school is a dead end, they quickly lose interest and often turn to risky behaviors in their search for self-affirmation. These students engage in a variety of risky behaviors, and are quickly identified as "at-risk youth." Among these risks is the initiation of sexual activity at an early age, with at-risk boys more likely to impregnate their partners and at-risk girls more likely to become pregnant than lower-risk teens who wait before becoming sexually active.[15] Poor achievement in school devalues their sense of self, while sexual activity, at least in the short term, enhances it.

Peer pressure, not to be overlooked, certainly exerts influence on adolescent self-esteem. As children develop into teenagers, peer pressure also becomes a factor in their decision-making. Adolescents have begun the process of breaking away from the emotional dependence they have had upon their parents. Teenagers have begun to examine and question their parents' values and views on morality and to entertain alternatives. Into this vacuum steps the peer group, whose values and opinions supplant to some extent those of parents and other adults. Social acceptance by one's peers is vastly more important to teenagers than approval by parents or other adults. A Harris organization poll found that social pressure is the most common reason adolescents give for entering into sexual activity rather than delaying it.[16] Peer pressure can also, however, be turned in favor of healthy behavior. If abstinence or condom use for safer sex can gain the endorsement of an adolescent group, the peer pressure can promote positive rather than negative activity.

ADOLESCENT SEXUAL BEHAVIOR

We have examined the attitudes adolescents may have toward their behavior, but what of that actual behavior itself? Based on the assumption that a mix of sexual activity and HIV is all that is necessary for AIDS to flourish, Karen Hein has identified three levels of risk for adolescents. The lowest level of risk involves those adolescents who are not at risk because they do not practice risk activities. The next level, moderate risk, involves those teenagers who are sexually active but so far have not encountered HIV. The first element for AIDS to thrive is present, but the second is still missing. The third and highest risk group contains those youth who are at immediate risk for HIV infection. They perform high-risk behaviors in the presence of the virus. Because HIV is a difficult virus to transmit, these teenagers are not necessarily HIV positive, but if they are not, it is only by chance.[17]

A number of outside influences contribute to adolescents' risky behavior. Risky sexual behavior in teenagers is, more often than not, related to other, more general antisocial behavior such as alcohol use, cigarette smoking, and drug use. Substance abuse in particular can bring about risky sex, and has been associated with lack of contraception and multiple partners. Individuals under the influence of drugs or alcohol often find their inhibitions lowered and their judgment affected. Contraception requiring direct action, such as putting on a condom or inserting a diaphragm or sponge, is easy to set aside during periods of compromised judgment and impaired motor skills.

Biological Susceptibility to HIV

Because of the biological changes that occur in adolescent females, HIV can be more infectious to them than to fully mature females. The reproductive systems of adolescent females are not yet fully developed, leaving vulnerabilities and susceptibilities to STDs through immature menstrual patterns and vaginal, cervical, and ovarian functions.[18] As HIV often follows the patterns of more established STDs, this information is disturbing enough, but other evidence exists to suggests that STDs, most particularly syphilis, can pave the way for HIV infection. Syphilis breaks down the skin and generates lesions, providing HIV with direct access to the bloodstream.[19] Adolescents tend not to seek out anonymous HIV tests, so an infectious individual can unwittingly infect others for quite some time before altering his or her behavior.

To make matters worse for adolescents, there are no clear guidelines for anonymous HIV testing by location. The laws in some states will allow anonymous testing for adolescents, while others demand parental notification. Not all states provide clear regulations and may leave teenagers desiring HIV tests in the dark as to whether their parents will later be informed of the results.[20] Under such questionable circumstances, adolescents are more likely to avoid these tests completely than to risk exposing their sexual activity to parents. It is such uninformed carriers of HIV who present the most serious threat in the spread of the virus.

Condom Use

Given that condoms present the most effective method of protection against either receiving or transmitting the virus, it is worth some small amount of space to explore the question of why their use is not more widespread. In all fairness, we must acknowledge that adolescents have actually increased their level of condom use in the last several years. Since the 1970s, reported condom use has increased by two or three times. In 1988, fifty-seven percent of surveyed males aged seventeen to nineteen reported using a condom the last time they had sexual intercourse.[21]

A profile of adolescents who are more likely than most to use condoms is fairly easy to sketch. Unlike the typical high-risk youth, probable condom users have a sense of themselves and of their future.[22] The type of relationship they are in also has some bearing on the prospect of whether or not they will use condoms. Teens in longer, established relationships perceive less need to use condoms than those in shorter, less serious relationships. The more casual the sexual activity, the more likely that condoms will be used consistently. Another factor that can affect condom use is the mutual desire of the partners to utilize them. If a young woman thinks her partner is open to the idea of condoms, she is more willing to make the suggestion and follow through consistently.[23] Of course, a profile of teens likely to use condoms also, through omission, reveals those who are not, and we are back to our old high-risk friends: adolescents who engage in sexual activity at an early age, who are sexually active with multiple partners, and who abuse substances likely to affect their judgment and ability to protect themselves.

Adolescents are at no loss to furnish extensive reasons why they do not use condoms. Like much of the larger society, teens simply find condoms distasteful. They claim condoms limit the pleasure of sexual intercourse and undermine its spontaneity. Further, elements distinctive to adolescents, such as the sense of invulnerability and the lack of abstract thinking, come into play as well. But more often than not, teenagers will provide very mundane reasons for avoiding condoms. One of the basic reasons teens fail to use condoms is simple embarrassment. Adolescents, both male and female, do not want to be seen purchasing condoms. Teenage women are afraid of the assumptions that will be made about them by those from whom they buy the condoms or who oversee the purchase. Further, if women have a condom ready and waiting for the possibility of sex, they fear their partner will see them as sexually experienced and vigorously chasing after sex.[24] Males, on the other hand, are simply uncomfortable dealing with their sexual activity in public view. Even though most adolescents seem to have no regret over their high level of sexual activity, they still carry a sense of guilt about it. When this embarrassment is added to the perceived inconvenience of having to go out of one's way to procure condoms in the first place, it results at best in indifference to the protection condoms offer and, at worst, in downright opposition to their use.

The element of partner trust is often central to the equation of using condoms. Teens of both genders fear that even to introduce the subject of condoms will be perceived by their partner as questioning that partner's honesty and sincerity within the relationship. A sexual history is still often regarded as a liability among adolescents, which echoes the guilt discussed earlier that is sometimes involved in buying condoms. Even if two adolescents start their sexual relationship using condoms, as that relationship shifts from short term to long term, which is generally considered longer than three months, and the two partners grow to trust each other, whether they have an exclusive sexual relationship or not, their reliance on condoms is greatly reduced. The desire to use condoms, no matter how strong it may have been at one time, more often than not disappears as a relationship continues.[25]

The issue of trust, however, is only a small part of the overall question of communication. Adolescent sexual partners, like many of their adult counterparts, do not talk before, during, or after their intimate encounters. Keeping mystery and ambiguity a part of the sexual relationship is a significant goal for adolescents as it makes the event itself more powerful, but also because it leaves a clear avenue for painless rejection if either partner chooses not to follow through to the expected intercourse.[26] The risk of rejection is very real for teens, as is the fear of being spurned by a partner. If either adolescent initiates a discussion of condoms, he or she is committing to the act of intercourse and leaving a huge hole through which to be repudiated by an ambivalent partner who may call off the entire encounter. If neither partner mentions condoms, the situation can progress slowly and seemingly spontaneously to its natural conclusion. If either partner does not desire to engage in coitus, a body softly turning away or a subtle shake of the head at the appropriate moment is a much more indirect and palatable refusal than an overt declaration before the intimacy has even begun. More adolescents may be carrying condoms in their wallets or purses, but many still do not know how to maneuver the emotional space between the wrapped condom waiting in their pocket and the open, unrolled condom ready for use.

A less frequent but no less significant reason condoms are avoided is the use of alcohol or drugs before or during sexual activity. As remarked upon earlier, the use of such substances lowers an adolescent's inhibitions and worries, making the need to employ a condom less compelling. In addition to changing a teenager's attitude about using condoms, even low levels of alcohol, marijuana, or other drugs can affect that individual's motor skills, making it more difficult to manipulate the condom. Even if they do not give up on the idea entirely, an even slightly tipsy couple runs the risk of putting the condom on incorrectly or not noticing a tear in the latex. Either circumstance can result in condom failure, the results of which could be either inconsequential or life-changing.

The most fundamental concern on the minds of sexually active teenagers, and most particularly females, is pregnancy. Compared to the worry of causing pregnancy or becoming pregnant, HIV and STDs are unimportant for teens. Unfortunately, if the main purpose of a couple's use of contraception is to protect themselves against pregnancy, there are any number of effective alternatives to condoms that do not protect against HIV. When asked about their use of condoms, adolescents who used other forms of birth control most often saw no reason to use condoms. If condoms are used in such circumstances at all, it is usually as a backup to birth control, not as a protection against HIV or STDs.[27]

Teenagers obviously present some very particular obstacles and challenges for AIDS educators. Treating them as young adults or as older children will not successfully prevent adolescents from becoming infected with HIV or, among those who are already infected or will become so sometime in the future, from spreading the virus. Educators know that they must approach a junior high school classroom differently than they would a high school classroom. This is even more true when comparing junior high and high school classes to elementary school, college, or university extension classrooms. Some strategies for teaching adolescents have proven much more successful than others. In the following chapters, we will explore and examine the teaching methods that have demonstrated themselves to have the greatest appeal to and best results with adolescents. By addressing teenagers today, we can help to prevent further complications in the AIDS crisis in the future.

2

Preparing an AIDS Education Program

Perhaps the first issue that teachers must address in planning and implementing a unit of AIDS education is how to relate to their principals and district officials. Some teachers may feel that they will not receive support for their efforts from their administrative superiors. While each situation will be different and teachers must ultimately trust their instincts and experience, it is possible that they can find more support from their principals and their superiors at the district level than they expect. AIDS is a problem that is recognized at every tier of education and government. In a national survey of district superintendents conducted fairly early in the AIDS pandemic, every participant agreed that AIDS education should be regularly taught in schools, and that schools should work with the health community to organize the best possible response for students.[1] Although there may be a feeling among teachers that school administrators are reluctant to lend their support to what may be unpopular AIDS education, and would rather stick with the politically safer "Just Say No" campaign, in reality there are few individuals who will argue that "Just Say No" is a viable response to the problem. The reason that school-based AIDS education appears to be slighted and that few comprehensive programs can be found may be as simple as the fact that no one has pushed forward to get things off the ground. The education system in this country has become so inundated with responsibilities at every level that AIDS education can easily become just one more bother. Teachers who are willing to leap in and attempt to meet the problem will, more likely than not, be welcomed by their district superintendents. School administrators have expressed interest in learning anything they can about how to address the educational challenge presented by AIDS, but have been discouraged by the overwhelming size of the problem and the amount of catching up that appears to be necessary within the educational community.[2]

GAINING COMMUNITY SUPPORT

Teachers who are able to gain the support of administrative officials, potentially up to the district level, will be in a good position to gauge community opinion and determine the location of potential support within the community. Every community is unique, and will offer different types of backing and opposition. Trying to construct an AIDS curriculum without public scrutiny will only result in frustration and defeat for anyone who attempts it. Any controversial content that teachers try to hide from those they fear will resist it will become public with much more negative publicity than it would have, had the teacher simply presented it openly to begin with. One of the first suggestions the Centers for Disease Control (CDC) made in its 1988 guidelines for effective AIDS education was that the "scope and content" of AIDS education should be "consistent with parental and community values," and determined locally.[3] Although this recommendation may seem somewhat constricting at first glance, it will actually save educators some major headaches down the road. By addressing potential problem areas openly, compromises can be reached and possible detractors can be brought into the fold early, changing their opposition to support. Rumors about "immoral" material and AIDS educators who encourage their students to become sexually active spread all too quickly if teachers allow even the slightest hint that they do not want parents involved in their classrooms.

If it is possible, administrative sources should make the planned educational program, resources, and materials available for review by interested members of the school board. Actual school board approval might be too time consuming or politically sensitive, but open disclosure and aboveboard behavior will avoid an ambush further down the line. No one, particularly political officials, likes to be surprised by controversy. As cannot be stressed enough, lining up support among allies on the school board before opposition is established will provide AIDS educators with a much stronger position if and when any resistance does arise.

Working with Parents

Even parents who might feel more comfortable teaching their children at home about AIDS know that they themselves do not have the information they need. As a result, parents are very likely to welcome a partnership with the schools to teach their children how to avoid HIV. The more candid that teachers become when discussing their instruction plans, the more trust they will be able to develop among parents and other community leaders. Although members of the religious right may protest loudly and ostentatiously, they will likely only speak for a small minority of the community. Openness with parents before the religious right or other opposition becomes a problem can be one of the most effective tools teachers and administrators use in blunting the effect of an adversarial situation. School systems in cities such as Baltimore that have attempted to deal openly and honestly with parents about their sexuality curricula have avoided the commotion and disturbances that have plagued the school systems in New York, Los Angeles, and Boston with great publicity. Even the United States military, in promoting HIV education for its personnel and their children stationed in Europe, suggested informing authority figures ("including parents," it was noted) in advance in order to avoid their opposition further down the line.[4]

Surveys of parents report overwhelming support for AIDS education, even to the point of approving explicit subject matter and materials for their children. Further, parents have also supported giving basic information about HIV and AIDS in early elementary school. Young students, a majority of parents feel, should be exposed to information about germs and disease and, as they get a bit older, to material addressing possible HIV infection in blood and the dangers of sharing needles. Finally, the majority of parents agree, preliminary facts about the connection of HIV and AIDS to sexual activity should be introduced to students as early as the fifth or sixth grade. A number of parents have also made known their desire to be a part of their children's education in these subjects.[5] If preliminary classes or less formal instruction for parents can be arranged as part of the campaign to build public support, more than just goodwill among parents will be created. Parents will have the opportunity and the means to supplement their children's education about HIV and AIDS at home while they pass along their own personal values and beliefs.

AIDS Education as a Component of Health and Sex Education

Another issue on which allies in administrative positions can offer assistance is in linking, wherever and whenever possible, instruction on HIV and AIDS with health and sexuality education. Most of the information about AIDS and the refusal skills that need to be taught in conjunction with it appear within the context of sexual activity. Outside that context, and the framework of health concerns that houses it, most of AIDS education will simply make little sense, and will leave slight if any impression on students. The Coalition of National Health Education Organizations offers three appropriate content areas in which to place instruction on HIV and AIDS: prevention and control of disease, prevention of substance use and abuse, and understanding human sexuality.[6] Introducing healthy habits to avoid risky behaviors and HIV infection in the context of a comprehensive health education curriculum that promotes other healthy habits is much more likely to be successful than presenting the AIDS material in a vacuum. Students need order in their learning, so they can determine how to put the separate pieces of information together so that it makes sense to their lives. If the information does not make sense, adolescents will be very unlikely to retain it. A random assembly with every other student in the school is much more likely to be disregarded by students than several class periods taught by their usual instructor. In addition, the presence of regular sex education in a school makes that school's likelihood of covering the topics of HIV and AIDS much stronger. An investigation of Louisiana schools found that the schools that did not provide regular sex education often failed to provide substantial instruction, if any, about HIV or AIDS.[7] Sex education classes allow a convenient avenue into the subject of STDs, and from there it is only a simple leap to HIV, AIDS, and various lessons in prevention. Although sex education is not absolutely necessary to the teaching of AIDS education, it makes the introduction of the material smoother and easier than it might otherwise be.

ABSTINENCE VERSUS SEXUAL ACTIVITY

A potential dilemma that can arise in the planning of AIDS education is the apparent struggle between promoting abstinence and teaching about responsible sexual activity. The first issue that must be addressed is to define these two positions as sympathetic to each other. The subject at hand is sexuality, which is a part of every individual's makeup. Abstinence is one way of approaching this ingredient of our human essence; sexual activity is another. Even within the area of sexual activity there are various permutations and methods of dealing with sexuality. Students' sexuality, like that of anyone else, cannot be denied. The sexual aspects of their humanity will always be present, and abstinence and activity are two different approaches to it.

Promoting Abstinence

Every responsible AIDS education program should include abstinence as a primary goal. A number of conservative pressure groups seem to fear that abstinence will be totally left out and scorned in a comprehensive education program that also includes information on safe sexual practices. Ignoring abstinence would be one of the most irresponsible acts that AIDS educators could commit. As conservatives correctly point out, abstinence is the only one-hundred-percent effective method of protecting oneself from HIV and AIDS. If a teenager abstains from sexual activity, that teenager is guaranteed not to become infected with HIV from sexual intercourse. To keep this information from students would be behavior that borders on the criminal. To cast the argument in moral and religious terms, however, will only muddy the educational waters. The subject at issue here is health education, not moral education. Health education is an objective subject. We can attain general agreement on which behaviors are healthy and which are hazardous to health. Morality is a subjective field. Two good, honest people can have a sincere disagreement over what constitutes moral, immoral, and amoral behavior. The AIDS education classroom must remain firmly in the realm of objective health education. Abstinence and active sexual lives are both equally possible decisions for young people to make.

One attainable goal teachers might set for themselves is to attempt to delay their students' sexual initiation, a target that has been met in programs focusing on substance abuse and pregnancy. Although several studies back this up, common sense alone tells us that the later an individual initiates sexual activity, the fewer sexual partners he or she will accumulate. If adolescents start later, they simply do not have as much time and as many opportunities to engage in sexual activity. Fewer partners and less sexual activity result in fewer chances to encounter HIV and become infected by it. Delaying the onset of sexual activity has been found to be easier than motivating adolescents to alter already existing behavior patterns. This fact must be used to support an early beginning to AIDS education in elementary school. It should not be misinterpreted as a strategy for high school teachers immersed in denial of their students' sexual activity. There is, obviously, no point in pretending that sexually active adolescents are not, in fact, engaging in sexual activities. All AIDS instruction must be grounded in reality. Teachers do not have to know the intimate details of their students' lives in order to assume that at least some of those students are adhering to a normal timetable of sexual activity. Avoiding the truth of teen behaviors that may make some teachers uncomfortable in discussing the subject of sexuality and AIDS will result in nothing but a disservice to students whose lives may genuinely be at risk. Giving up on certain teens as unchangeable will likewise result in selling their potential short. Research has shown that even the most hard-core IV drug user can change when he or she is willing to make the effort. Giving up on these teens can cause them to give up on themselves, which almost certainly locks them into their current behaviors.

Safer Sexual Activities

Once AIDS educators have acknowledged that some of their students are sexually active, they must not encourage these students to revert to abstinence. Advocating "secondary virginity," as it is called in some programs, may comfort the teachers, but it will have very little effect on the students. Sexually active students generally do not want to give up the "advances" toward adulthood they feel they have made. If AIDS units must have such goals in order to quell community concern or assuage vocal parents, they should be only one factor of the educational material. AIDS instructors who ignore their students' high-risk sexual activity do so not only at their own risk, but at the risk of those very students' lives.

Therefore, in addition to a focus on abstinence, responsible sexual activity must also be included. This information will not give students ideas they have not already formulated from watching television, going to movies, reading magazines, and even seeing billboards that use sexuality to sell their products. Instead, AIDS education will teach students how to accept and process that information and react to it in a responsible manner. The hesitancy of some constituencies to allow frank discussion of sexuality and in the process to save students' lives must be overcome or, at the very least, set aside. Information is not a dangerous resource for adolescents, and all pertinent information must be included.

Addressing Condoms

The teaching of condom use will very likely be a point of contention during the planning of an AIDS education program. While it may be easy to understand the hesitation of some community members to welcome education about condom use into the schools, it is a subject whose relevance and necessity cannot be understated. Teachers justifying the inclusion of condoms should cite the esteemed British medical journal *The Lancet*, which editorialized in 1993 that only marginally increasing the levels of condom use among the population would greatly inhibit the spread of HIV. "If condoms were used by 40% of heterosexuals, 60% of homosexuals, and 87% of prostitutes, there would be a striking reduction in the number of cases of AIDS over the next 20-25 years. Exclusion of condom use in this model produced an epidemic approaching that of developing countries."[8] Dire numbers such as these demand that the proper use of condoms be fully addressed in a responsible AIDS education program. It will not be enough for the teacher to simply gloss over the idea of condoms, mentioning that their use helps limit HIV infection. Adolescents need specific instruction on precisely how, when, and why condoms should be used.

Reducing Risk

Although the highest-risk students may be harder to reach, they are certainly not beyond the help that educators can offer. Sexually active students can be encouraged to try less risky sexual behavior that does not escalate to the level where condoms are necessary, such as hugging and kissing, sensual touching, masturbation, and, if intercourse does remain a possibility, consistent condom use during intercourse. By taking an active approach to these and other less risky behaviors, at-risk students can lower their hazard. Attitudes that favor higher risk should also be targeted for education. Many adolescent girls can benefit from improving their communication skills to avoid sexual intercourse or at least to insist on the protection of condoms and spermicides when engaging in such activity. Adolescent males can also be exposed to the ideas that unprotected penetrative intercourse is not the be-all and end-all of sexual activity. Other actions, such as those referred to above, can be equally satisfying aspects of sexual behavior. Students at high risk can learn that they have the ultimate control over their own behavior. They can be taught how to avoid pressure exerted on them by themselves, their friends, and their partners.

Another way of reaching at-risk students can be to target their concern over pregnancy. For the most part, teenage females obviously do not want to become pregnant, and teenage males do not want to cause their partner to become pregnant. Although the consequences of unintended pregnancy are much higher for females than males, male concern should not be understated. Many, although of course not all, of the methods sexual partners can use to prevent pregnancy also prevent the transmission of HIV. Any of the previously listed lower-risk sexual practices also offer protection against pregnancy. Anything these students learn about reproductive health will be to their benefit, and any method that educators can use to involve their students in the material will be worthwhile. Sometimes merely arousing students' interest in school and helping them to become more interested and receptive to any subject matter, not simply health or AIDS education, can cause students to lower their level of risk behavior. Also, as is no secret to junior high and high school educators, teenagers are heavily influenced in terms of attitudes and behaviors by their peers. If the perception of peer norms can be nudged away from the glamorization and expectation of risk behavior, then the behavior itself will be modified as well. Peer pressure can be used to encourage safer, lower-risk activities, sexual or otherwise, just as effectively as it often seems to sanction dangerous, high-risk behaviors.

Devising a unit to address HIV and AIDS can be particularly tricky because of the nature of human sexuality itself. As we have said, knowledge about HIV and AIDS is not enough to sway adolescents away from high-risk sexual activity. The sex drives of teenagers and adults alike are not fully understood or, at the very least, are not the focus of great agreement among educators, their overseeing school boards, and their communities. One's sexuality certainly involves a number of psychological factors in different patterns and quantities, depending upon the individual. These factors cannot be denied by parents or teachers in formulating a strategy for AIDS education. An effective AIDS education unit will include the psychosocial elements that aid in determining a person's sexual attitudes and behaviors. Different individuals react to sex in different ways, and as much as possible, these reactions should be taken into account by teachers. The relationships that lead to sexual activity and the emotional and psychological reactions both participants experience should be included in all educational efforts. These relationships and reactions are different for adolescents and for adults, and AIDS educators must take that into consideration.

In light of the physical and psychological ravages that HIV and AIDS can inflict upon infected individuals, it is also important that educators not neglect the positive aspects of sexuality. Sexual activity is not a negative, damaging experience that must be avoided at all costs. To paint it as a frightening, dirty, immoral act cheapens both the instructor and the students. Given the ambivalence many people feel about adolescent sexuality, painting an accurate picture of sex at this age, balancing both positive and negative aspects, can be a very tall order.

TEACHER PREPARATION

In preparing curricula and instruction about HIV and AIDS, teachers are likely to confront many more issues, both public and private, than they have been used to. A much higher level of research, sensitivity, and even personal soul-searching is often necessary in this subject area than in more traditional subjects such as math and grammar. Teachers should not underestimate the amount of preparation that will be necessary to successfully formulate an effective AIDS curriculum. They are the linchpins of successful AIDS education, and must take their charge very seriously. District supervisors in one survey were quick to acknowledge that the success of their

AIDS education programs was largely due to the preparation and sensitivity of their teachers. A minority of supervisors, those unhappy with the results of their district's AIDS education efforts, placed that failure directly at the feet of the teachers, who, supervisors felt, were not adequately prepared for the task at hand.[9] It is entirely true that the success or failure of a proposed AIDS education curriculum may be determined before anyone, students or teachers, sets foot in a classroom. Even more than most subject areas, AIDS education can stand or fall with the decisions teachers make about which information, activities, and ideas to include in the curriculum. Different teachers will choose to stress some facets of the AIDS crisis over others; such choices will determine how helpful the curriculum will be to the students it attempts to influence.

Teachers must become familiar with the vast information available about HIV and AIDS. Although no one expects public school AIDS instructors to stay on top of every journal article published and every new development announced, teachers must realize that the field of AIDS information shifts quickly. What we understood about HIV and AIDS a year ago is not necessarily what we believe about them today. Teachers must gain an introduction to AIDS material, and then supplement that from time to time with short updates. Also, teachers and administrators must be aware that information concerning AIDS is not strictly limited to medical and scientific facts. Social factors that influence the transmission of AIDS, such as beliefs and attitudes surrounding the virus, the syndrome, and, rightly or wrongly, the groups associated with them, are at least as worthy of educators' attention as how HIV leads to AIDS.

The Centers for Disease Control identifies some areas that teachers should try to include in their training. First is the appropriate medical and scientific knowledge. This would include modes of transmission, protection against transmission, and any useful statistical information, such as the most recent numbers for heterosexual transmission. Secondly, teachers must gain skills and knowledge related to current thinking about the best methods of providing AIDS education to their students. AIDS education for school-age children and teenagers remains in its infancy, and much of the education theory that surrounds it is little more than speculation. As more and more schools adopt and evaluate AIDS education programs, more and more hard, proven knowledge and experience will be available to teachers. The third area of useful teacher training is a survey or overview of available methods and materials concerning education about AIDS. New texts and techniques are cropping up regularly, and teachers need some sort of review to keep up. There is no reason to stick with last year's guides and methodology if this year's have proven to be more effective.

Psychological Issues

Teachers should not underestimate the helpfulness of addressing the psychosocial issues that they themselves will face in presenting material about HIV and AIDS. To provide the most effective program, AIDS instructors must provide as open a discussion as possible. When students are encouraged to ask any questions at all or make any observation that they may have on this topic, they are likely to bring up unexpected subjects that teachers and fellow classmates might find uncomfortable. Teachers must go to whatever lengths are necessary to be prepared for such instances. Also, because HIV infection carries such grave consequences, instructors must be aware of how individual students are reacting to the material. Some students may have worries about family members or friends who are or they fear may be HIV positive. A few students are likely even to carry the fear that they themselves are already infected or heavily at risk. Because the consequences involved in HIV infection include early death, AIDS instructors must have a much higher level of sensitivity for such possibilities than is necessary for instructors of math or grammar, for instance. Any training that will prepare teachers for such situations should be pursued.

Personal Prejudices and Biases

Training should also be sought to help teachers overcome any prejudices or biases they discover within themselves. Almost everyone has preconceived notions that somehow relate to the issue of HIV and AIDS, whether that is a personal discomfort with homosexuality, an unease with teenage sexual activity, an anxiety over personal contact with HIV-positive individuals, or any one of a number of issues that could come between a teacher and his or her students. As recommended earlier, AIDS instructors need to acknowledge and confront these biases and the inhibitions they may create in order to offer effective HIV and AIDS instruction. Students have an uncanny knack of recognizing a teacher's soft spot and exploiting it to their advantage. Before a teacher can provide the open discussion necessary to AIDS education, he or she must be able to overcome personal bias. This can be effectively addressed in teacher training sessions or the possible counseling that might accompany them. In one survey, district supervisors appeared to be very reluctant to acknowledge the need to create a comfortable learning environment, which might suggest a general disinterest in presenting any material other than the straight facts about HIV and AIDS, an educational approach proven to be ineffective in this subject area.[10] Teacher training should encourage teachers to establish a comfortable learning environment for their students and provide useful techniques through which it can be achieved.

EDUCATIONAL STRATEGIES

As much as is possible, AIDS education should be a very positive situation for educators and students. Affirmative attitudes about sex, life, and health are all possible through effective instruction. One group of educators developing an AIDS intervention program for youth in residential centers suggests three primary components of useful AIDS education. First of all, they see a clarification of personal issues surrounding their students as important. These issues would include values, ambition for the future, and positive life options. Helping students understand that their lives in the present and the future are valuable and important will help them take their current decisions more seriously. Secondly, the educators must enhance their students' perspective on preventing AIDS, allowing it to become more positive and affirmative. If adolescents perceive HIV to be easily avoidable, they will be much more willing to make the effort necessary to avoid it. Finally, after two attitudinal components, the third element is much more practical. The skills necessary to successfully prevent HIV infection must be nurtured within students. The skills can be purely functional, such as how to use a condom properly, or communicative, such as how to tactfully but firmly refuse intercourse.[11] In many ways, successful AIDS education boils down to simple points such as these. When students display such a blatant need for training in areas that so powerfully affect their lives, in many ways it falls to the educator to provide that training.

Language

Teachers must be prepared to talk plainly about sex and AIDS with their students, using the terms that students commonly use and have become comfortable with. In using slang and sometimes impolite language, students frequently test their teachers for knowledge and reaction. They may indeed be trying to embarrass their teachers. Teachers in such situations who reveal their embarrassment will lose credibility in discussing these subjects. Instructors who are able to look back to their own adolescent years will remember the feeling that adults "just don't get it." Teenagers feel that adults have no understanding of what their attitudes and desires are. Teachers who can relate to and empathize with teenagers and convey those feelings to their students will prove much more effective in discussing these important subjects than teachers who remain at a distance from their students. Troubled students will sometimes even approach their sympathetic teachers with problems or questions, providing one of the most powerful opportunities these teachers will ever encounter for teaching about sex and AIDS.

Although some teachers may be comfortable using graphic slang terms describing body parts, their functions, and other activities in individual conversations with students, many teachers are embarrassed to bring them into the classroom. As much as possible, this embarrassment must be overcome. There are two main reasons for this. First of all, many students simply do not understand clinical, scientific language for sexual subjects. For instance, the term "penile-vaginal intercourse" might as well be another language to many students. Without a doubt, the vast majority of students will recognize and understand the activity referred to, but not under that name. If the only words students might understand are "putting the cock in the pussy," the instructor must use them, at least as a starting point. Even if the teacher attempts to move toward more clinical language later in the unit, students must still be made to realize that "penis" is the same as "cock" and "vagina" is the proper word for "pussy." Such plain, explicit language may be among the most controversial elements of an AIDS education unit, but it is also one of the most important. If students do not understand the basic language and concepts of the subject matter, they will not even begin to comprehend any of the material presented, let alone retain enough of it to change their behavior. If at all possible, this must be an area where teachers compromise as little as possible. Graphic language may initially be uncomfortable for teachers and maybe even for a few students, but as the language becomes more and more commonplace, this discomfort will fade somewhat.

Skills Training

After an informational foundation of AIDS vocabulary, actions, and functions has been achieved, teachers can move on to the skills-training elements of AIDS education. The skills that students should be taught range from accurately perceiving their level of vulnerability to HIV infection, to recognizing a high-risk situation and, in order to either avoid it completely or lessen the potential threat, to openly communicating and negotiating their desire to practice safer sex in an intimate situation. Results such as these are the most obvious outcomes that educators would like to achieve through AIDS education, and they are actually quite attainable.

Beyond achieving this openness, students must also learn not to fear confrontation if it is necessary. To navigate the perilous territory of AIDS and STDs, students must gain the capacity to refuse others in the case of unsafe sexual situations, to insist on certain circumstances or actions such as the use of condoms when the safety of a sexual situation is unclear, and to handle the consequences of these situations if immediate agreement and compliance are not the result. Although perhaps easy to control on paper and in theory, sexual relationships can become very traumatic, and the physical danger can become more immediate than the risk of infection by HIV. Confrontational sexual predicaments are difficult for everyone, but they are particularly difficult for adolescents, who are seeking acceptance and approval. Teenagers are unlikely to stand their ground and protect themselves if that means potential exclusion and isolation from friends and peers. The phrase "go along to get along" is one that many teens live by. To gain the strength of self-image and confidence needed to assert these life-saving skills is one of the most important functions AIDS education can perform. If students take with them nothing else but these skills, the time and effort taken to prepare and present AIDS education will be worthwhile.

Hand in hand with these communication skills must come decision-making skills that enable adolescents to recognize and sum up the risk level inherent in a given situation and make a careful, deliberate decision about how to proceed. If communication skills break down in a sexual situation, and a partner absolutely refuses to use a condom under any circumstances, the teenager at risk must be able to make the responsible decision to refuse participation in the sexual activity and hold firmly to that decision. But decision-making skills should come into play even before such urgent decisions need to be made. Decision-making skills will help students consider who their friends are and who they want them to be. Students will be able to use their skills to recognize situations that initially appear quite innocent but have the potential to turn risky, and then to make a decision on how far to pursue the situation. If adolescents set firm limits at the beginning of a situation and stick with them throughout, they will be much less likely to find themselves in a hazardous predicament that calls for urgent decision-making.

These skills are fairly easy to identify, but, just as knowledge alone is not enough to sway adolescents from their risky behavior, teaching how to recognize these skills and addressing how and when to use them falls short of influencing behavior change. Teachers must employ methods that bring their students into the act of using and practicing these skills. Modeling and role-playing are the most effective teaching techniques to accomplish this. Teachers, working with their assistants or other teachers, can demonstrate the nuts and bolts of how people must actually utilize these skills in real-life situations. Students can then play roles with each other in a variety of situations to practice these skills before needing to employ them in hazardous situations. Basketball players do not only practice their foul shots in the middle of a game; they stand at the free throw line for long periods of time shooting one foul shot after another, practicing when the pressure is off, so that when they face the high pressure of a game potentially won or lost on their basket, they will be ready. Adolescents are like basketball players. If they are given the hands-on opportunity to practice these skills in the low-pressure, friendly environment of the classroom, they will be much more likely to remember the skills and use them when the consequences are greater.

Interactive methods that allow students to take part in their education can be adapted to material about AIDS quite easily. Video tapes, peer education, role-playing, and teaching games can all prove useful as teachers delve deeper into the subject matter. If the classroom looks interesting and appealing through the use of posters, brochures, and pictures of relevant sports stars or other celebrities, the students will find their interest piqued and their attention focused. Teachers can also make the study of AIDS and HIV more personal by bringing in AIDS patients or HIV-positive individuals to talk with the class or to make a presentation. The closer these individuals are in age, class, and ethnicity to the students, the more the students may be able to relate to their situations, but a particularly forceful and effective speaker of any age or background can overcome such concerns. A guest like this in the classroom can help to personalize HIV and AIDS and can encourage students to make changes in their own behaviors.

Teaching AIDS in the Multicultural Classroom

In the AIDS classroom, teachers may find the need to balance a number of attitudes and outlooks simultaneously. While it is easy to assign high risk only to particular groups of people who engage in certain types of activities, such as homosexual men or highly promiscuous teens, teachers must be sure that they do not stigmatize those groups and, by extension, exclude any students in the classroom who may privately belong to such groups. One of the hallmarks of adolescence is struggling with one's sexuality. Some teenagers may engage in intimate same-sex activity while denying the possibility of being homosexual because of the social stigmas that are often associated with such an identity. Even in an open and nonjudgmental discussion, these youths might hear the word *homosexual* in a classroom discussion of AIDS, refuse to acknowledge that the term has anything to do with them, and ignore any cautionary advice or information that the teacher or other students impart about safe-sex activity. If the instructor or discussion leader offers derogatory or inflammatory views and opinions about homosexuality, there is absolutely no chance that these youth will reveal anything of themselves to the class, and chances are high that they would not even admit their activities and thoughts to themselves. Also, some students will have family members or friends who are among these groups, and stigmatizing material presented by a teacher can easily generate shame on their part or fear that their loved ones may become or already are infected with HIV and may die as a result. Either of these responses can undermine a student's response to the instruction. If teachers do not strive to embrace diversity in their approach to AIDS education, they will at the very least stimulate negative views among their students of persons infected with HIV or diagnosed with AIDS, and may very possibly force any students with homosexual leanings to push their feelings and activities underground, hiding them even from themselves, and condemning such students to high-risk behavior they refuse to acknowledge.

Another facet of the presentational openness that teachers must strive to achieve and maintain is that of ethnic and cultural diversity. Virtually every classroom will be composed of a heterogenous mixture of students. Teachers must be aware of the various social and cultural strands that bind together in their classrooms, and must keep the educational approach inclusive enough to embrace all students. Factors such as economic realities, religious beliefs, gender differences, and ethnic and cultural values will be different among most groups of students, and will sway their thinking and their reactions to the material addressed by AIDS education efforts. The methodology and substance of AIDS education embraced by teachers must be concocted in such a way as to address the multicultural classroom. Certain groups will practice some sexual activities more than other groups. For instance, because virginity is so important to Hispanic culture, some Hispanic girls indulge in anal sex, thus achieving the excitement of sexual intercourse but maintaining their virgin status. Sensitivity among members of this cultural group to the subject of anal intercourse would be higher than it might be to those in other cultural groups. These are precisely the sorts of differences to which teachers should become sensitive. What might be effective educational techniques for one group of students could prove relatively ineffective for another. Teachers must juggle the interests and perspectives of the adolescents in their classrooms in order to give each individual student the full value of the information and skills being presented.

Achieving universal interest and attention is also important when it comes to the skills portions of AIDS units. Various cultural and social groups will react differently to the diverse skills offered, with some skills striking greater resonance with particular groups than with others. Whatever methods a teacher employs to keep his or her students interested in learning and practicing these skills is positive. The proper balancing act for a particular classroom is something only an individual teacher can know.

Do Not Try to Scare Your Students

An important limit that AIDS educators must place upon themselves is not to fall into the use of scare tactics to motivate their students. Adolescents see through such maneuvers almost immediately, and are quite unlikely to fall for them. One of the most difficult and frustrating aspects of developing an AIDS prevention program is the realization that adolescents do not take death seriously enough to fear it. Death is an abstraction. Teachers, older and perhaps having experienced the death of loved ones, find this hard to reconcile, but they must reflect on their own teenage years to remember how obscure the idea of death was to them. Some adolescents may have been touched by the death of a grandparent or a pet, but many adolescents have never seen death firsthand at all. For those who have, it is a huge jump from the death of an elderly grandparent to recognize their own mortality. Other people die, but teenagers do not expect it will happen to them.

Instructional Time

Complete research has not yet been conducted to determine just how much time is necessary for an effective AIDS education program. We know that one hour is not enough. One week still runs short of time. Perhaps the most important element of AIDS education on the part of teachers is perseverance. As already stated, AIDS education sets out to change habits and attitudes. Dieters and smokers can testify to the amount of work necessary to maintain the staying power of behavior changes. Based on comparisons with other health-related curricula and their duration, fifteen or more hours of instruction seems an effective duration for an isolated program of AIDS education. If the material is taught as part of a comprehensive health and sex education curriculum, somewhat less than a full fifteen hours need be committed specifically to the subject of HIV and AIDS.[12] This fifteen hours is what would be necessary to launch a program of AIDS education for older students. If such material were presented at an earlier age to younger children, students would be able to become exposed to it in bits and pieces. In other words, the purpose of the initial, fifteen-hour, AIDS curriculum is essentially to make up for lost instructional time. After students have completed an initial HIV and AIDS curriculum, frequent refresher courses, one or two hours a semester, perhaps, would be necessary to reinforce the knowledge, skills, and behavioral aspects of AIDS education.

Habits are not changed from a single exposure to an AIDS curriculum, not even a fifteen-hour one. Perseverance is the key to successful behavior modification. According to educators, the single greatest weakness in existing AIDS education programs is insufficient instructional time.[13] To make the effort to develop an AIDS curriculum and to organize school and community support behind it, only to undermine its educational benefits by cutting short instructional time, would be a disservice to students who need the training and guidance an AIDS program would provide, and a tragedy for those who later become infected with HIV and contract AIDS for want of effective preventive strategies. In some cases, however, it might be effective to make up for less instructional time by dividing students into smaller classes. If a class consists of fifteen to twenty students, each student will be able to receive more individual attention from the instructor than in a class consisting of thirty or more students. Also, less time needs to be set aside for role-playing activities if there are fewer students to participate.

Resistance to Openness

Of course, one hazard comes with frank, open talk, whether in the classroom or at extracurricular activities: some people do not like it. One young fifth grader on the way to an AIDS assembly told her teacher that she hoped she would not hear a lot about sex, because that kind of talk always made her angry. This type of attitude is not as unusual as it may sound. A number of people are made angry, uncomfortable, embarrassed, or upset by sexual discussion. People who have such reactions may simply tune out any material that teachers present. Whatever the logical basis students may devise for tuning out information about AIDS, such as the fact that they are not in a risk group, that they are not yet sexually active, or that they are careful in choosing their partners, teachers must not allow them to ignore this important material. Students who tune out the curriculum will not be easy to spot, so teachers should pay attention to every student whenever possible. These defense mechanisms can be overcome if teachers acknowledge the various views of sexuality held by individual students throughout the classroom. If the views of students who would otherwise utilize avoidance techniques to elude AIDS-protection training are validated before the AIDS curriculum begins, teachers will have a good chance of reaching every student in their classroom.[14]

Tolerance

Teachers must also be sure to include various aspects of the social issues surrounding HIV and AIDS in their presentation. Because of the circumstances surrounding the introduction of HIV to this country, the issue of homosexuality remains an integral part of the dialogue surrounding AIDS. It is not uncommon for young people struggling to understand their emerging sexual feelings to develop feelings of homophobia. Although the identification of AIDS as a gay disease has long since been shown to be false, many heterosexual individuals feel invulnerable to HIV simply because they are not gay. Furthermore, adolescent prejudice against homosexuals has been linked to a lack of intention among these adolescents to shift from high-risk to low-risk behavior. As this prejudice rises, teens' perception of their own risk of HIV infection drops.[15] It is entirely possible that teaching awareness of homosexuality can not only bring about tolerance but may help students to better recognize their own level of risk.

Simple risk reduction, however, is not the only reason that tolerance should be a part of AIDS education. Sensitivity and compassion toward others is always an aspiration of education. Understanding of those outside ourselves and empathy for their feelings and reactions helps us to become fuller, more humane individuals. We can sometimes gain insight into ourselves and the situations we face if we are able to glimpse, even for a moment, the inner lives and feelings of those around us. In the case of HIV and AIDS, however, when we cultivate our sensitivity toward those already infected with HIV and the uncertain future they face and our compassion for those already suffering through the ravages of AIDS itself, we grow as individuals. Gaining a perception of the threat that the virus and disease can pose to us is also a likely effect of this realization, but it is not our primary goal. The more we can relate to people who have become infected with HIV, the deeper our understanding of the serious nature of the virus and its implications for our society will grow.

STUDENT DISCLOSURES

As an unexpected result of the in-depth exploration of sexuality provided by a program of AIDS education, students might reveal confidential information to their teacher or even to the class as a whole. Although teachers cannot anticipate which students might disclose what information when, they must do what they can to be prepared. Teachers who present AIDS education to a number of classes should expect at some time to be confronted with the issue of child sexual abuse. It is estimated that between twenty-eight and thirty-six percent of children below the age of fourteen have experienced some sort of sexual abuse in their lifetime.[16] There is very little an individual teacher can do in such a situation, and AIDS instructors would be advised not to attempt to deal with the issue alone. Instead, teachers should have at hand referral information for abuse services that employ professionals who specialize in handling this type of delicate matter. It might even be useful for teachers to make contact with these services to let them know that such referrals might be coming.

A second disclosure that might be made by students is that of homosexuality. Gay or lesbian students have particular issues that face them in school, such as homophobia and the lack of appropriate information or misinformation regarding their sexuality. If homosexual youth feel unwelcome and alienated in school, they are likely to ignore information offered through AIDS education. If a student reveals to a teacher that he or she is gay or lesbian, that teacher is advised to refer the student to community services able to address the unique difficulties relating to HIV or sexuality in general that young homosexuals experience. Teachers should be careful, however, not to become too enthusiastic in identifying and revealing students they believe to be gay or lesbian. Disclosure of a student's sexual identity before that student is ready to be revealed can result in severe problems for the student. It is common for teenagers to explore and struggle with their sexual identity. Many of the surface aspects of sexuality are new at this age, and teenagers need to discover and accept whatever sexual yearnings come naturally to them. For a teacher to come in and circumvent this process by assigning a sexual identity to a student before it is fully formed can be psychologically dangerous for the student. This is a discussion that must certainly be initiated by the student. Teachers must be sure that they demonstrate an openness and willingness to talk about such matters in confidence. If students feel that a teacher is approachable, they will feel much more confident in seeking out that teacher's help when they are ready.

3

Facts and Information

Although we have often repeated the truth that information alone is not sufficient to change attitudes, facts and details do provide the basis for any education about AIDS. Students must know how HIV is spread and how it is not. They must know how the virus's spread can be prevented and avoided. Although this new knowledge will likely not cause them to rethink many of their activities, it does open the door for teachers to later influence that desired change in behavior. The first thing that a teacher must do in presenting an AIDS education unit is to give students the facts. This chapter will outline the facts that are necessary for successful AIDS education. The next chapter will discuss in broad terms which information and concepts are appropriate for which ages. In this chapter, information pertinent to AIDS education will be presented in one piece, regardless of its appropriateness for various ages. Teachers can sift through this information and, in conjunction with the guidelines for age-appropriate content in Chapter 4, come to their own conclusions as to what is suitable for their own particular classes. Some information will be useful for younger students, some only for older students. Because each classroom is unique, only individual teachers can properly determine what is relevant to their students and what is not. Each teacher knows his or her class better than anyone else, and is the best judge of what particular students are prepared to hear and understand.

The biological and medical facts of AIDS are relatively straight-forward, if somewhat uncomfortable to discuss. Because teachers can fall back into a familiar lecture mode with this material, it tends to make up the bulk of existing AIDS education programs in the country. These facts simply provide the basis for changing students' attitudes, and should by no means be considered ends in themselves. In fact, the primary function of this information is to provide a con-text for the skills component to come. Teachers should also remind themselves to involve their students in this material as much as pos-sible. When a teacher is ill at ease, it is easier to fall into comfortable patterns of speaking before the class than to seek out innovative methods of capturing students' imaginations. Possible class activities will be provided in Chapter 5.

The facts presented here relate strictly to HIV and AIDS. Some students who have not had basic health courses may need more background on diseases or viruses than will be provided here. Such information can be found in virtually any health or medical text-book. Teachers are advised to seek out such texts if they need more general information on infectious diseases and viruses.

WHAT IS AIDS?

The term "AIDS" stands for *Acquired Immune Deficiency Syndrome*. Each of these words has a meaning that helps explain what AIDS is and how it works. *Acquired* refers to something that people get from outside themselves. Anything that people have that they were not born with has somehow been acquired by them. Since people are only born with their bodies, their hands, feet, eyes, noses, mouths, and every other part of their body are natural and are not acquired. Some diseases, such as diabetes, are hereditary and are passed through families, from parents to children before birth, and are therefore not acquired. AIDS is not hereditary, but it is transmitted from one person to another through various means.

The definition of the word *immune* is invulnerable or protected. If something is immune, then it cannot be hurt or defeated. The body has an immune system that fights off diseases such as the flu, colds, and other illnesses. If the body's immune system is working properly, a person may get ill with some sort of sickness but will later get better. The immune system battles disease by creating antibodies to fight the source of the disease and ultimately to get rid of it entirely. Our immune system is what keeps us from getting sick all the time from invading germs and viruses.

Unfortunately, the next word in AIDS is *deficiency*. *Deficiency* means not enough of something, a shortage. If a student fails a test, that means he or she has a deficiency, a lack, of knowledge on the subject. In the term "AIDS," *deficiency* is teamed up with *immune*, meaning that the body does not have enough immunity to fight off germs and diseases effectively. Viruses invade the body from the outside, and under normal circumstances the immune system is strong enough to fight most of them off completely. We come into contact with a number of germs and viruses every day, and the reason that we are not sick all the time is that our immune system keeps us healthy. If that immune system is not as strong as it should be, if it is deficient, then our bodies become like an open door to any number of dangerous invaders.

The final word, *syndrome*, refers to a group of symptoms that combine to demonstrate a particular condition or disease. In the case of AIDS, these symptoms include the presence of HIV in the body and the deficient immune system discussed above, as well as a number of opportunistic infections, such as Kaposi's sarcoma, pneumocystis carinii pneumonia (PCP), and lymphoma, that take advantage of the body's weak state to get a foothold. When enough of these symptoms get together in one body, the diagnosis of AIDS is made.

The term "AIDS," all of these words—Acquired Immune Deficiency syndrome—together, refers to a group of symptoms that people get from somewhere outside themselves and that weaken the body's ability to defend itself against diseases. With this kind of explanation, it is obvious why AIDS is such a dangerous and deadly matter.

WHAT IS HIV?

Obvious questions that students might ask at this point are: "Does AIDS infect people? Do people catch AIDS?" The answer, of course, is no. AIDS does not infect people, but HIV does. HIV stands for *human immunodeficiency virus*. *Human*, obviously, means that this is a virus that affects humans, or people. It does not infect animals, although there are some similar but not identical viruses that do infect animals. HIV does not infect dogs, cats, fish, hamsters, mosquitos, or any other animal students can think of. Therefore, HIV-positive people have acquired HIV only from other people. The second word, *immunodeficiency*, combines two of the words used in "AIDS," and means a weak defense system for the body. *Virus*, of course, is the name for a microscopic agent that causes disease. Students will likely be familiar with viruses as the cause of colds, chicken pox, measles, and the flu. As we know, viruses such as these can be passed from person to person through the air or through shared foods and drinks. HIV cannot survive when exposed to the air, so such contagion is not possible.

When someone is infected with HIV, the virus will begin to break down the body's immune system. After the initial HIV infection, many people remain healthy and free of opportunistic diseases for ten years or more. The immune system puts up a valiant resistance from the time of initial infection, but with the onset of opportunistic disease the virus ultimately overwhelms the body's ability to fight back.[1] In rough terms, the virus invades white blood cells called T cells. T cells, as integral parts of the immune system, help the body coordinate its defenses against germs and viruses. HIV attacks the T cells, incapacitating them so they can no longer protect the body. A healthy body generally has between eight hundred and twelve hundred T cells per cubic millimeter of blood. This number is called the "T-cell count." As T cells become infected, this count gradually drops. A T-cell count of two hundred qualifies an individual for an official diagnosis of AIDS.[2] Someone with such a T-cell count of two hundred, however, may not have any other AIDS-related symptoms, and may continue to appear perfectly healthy. Unless this person has a suspicion that he or she has been infected with HIV, he or she may have no reason to have his or her T cells counted. Even though such a person would be diagnosed with AIDS, he or she could potentially remain completely oblivious to that reality.

Because so much time usually elapses between the initial HIV infection and any obvious symptoms of AIDS, it is impossible to identify people's HIV status by looking at them. People who are HIV-positive, as well as many people who have actually been diagnosed with AIDS, look just as healthy as people who have never been exposed to HIV. In fact, without an AIDS test, someone who has been infected with HIV will be unaware of the infection. Therefore, the virus can be transmitted from one unsuspecting person to another. People do not need to know they have been infected with HIV in order to pass it on.

HOW DOES SEX TRANSMIT HIV?

Transmission of HIV is both very easy and very difficult. It is easy because there are very specific avenues through which HIV can be passed. HIV lives and thrives in human bodily fluids, and when these fluids are passed from one person to another, HIV can be passed right along with them. The four bodily fluids that carry HIV in a high enough concentration to infect others are blood; semen, which includes preejaculatory fluid, the male secretion that precedes semen and is also sometimes known as precome; vaginal fluids; and breast milk.[3] For our purposes, we will refer to these four as *high-risk bodily fluids*. Trace amounts of HIV can be found in other bodily fluids, such as tears or saliva, as well, but doctors have never recorded a large enough amount of the virus in such fluids to successfully make it infectious to another person.[4]

For HIV to be successfully transmitted, it must move from the bloodstream of one person to the bloodstream of another. When students stop to consider this fact, they will realize that this is a tricky proposition. An obvious method of transmission, especially for children and younger teenagers, is to transfer blood while becoming "blood brothers." The whole point of this ritual is to share blood, so if one participant is HIV-positive, the other participants will be exposed to the virus. Without a deliberate effort, however, it is more difficult for a person to exchange blood with someone else. Helping an HIV-positive person with a bloody nose, for example, does not put the helper at risk unless that helper also has open cuts in the skin through which the blood can enter. Skin is an excellent barrier to HIV. The virus cannot pass through the skin or its pores to get to the bloodstream.

The most obvious focus of HIV transmission is, of course, through sexual activity. The term "sexual activity," however, can encompass everything from romantically holding hands to vaginal or anal intercourse. Students will want to know what is risky behavior and what is not. The obvious answer, of course, is any activity that involves the possible exchange of any of the four high-risk bodily fluids listed above. HIV can enter the body through actual cuts in the skin or through mucous membranes found in the mouth, throat, vagina, rectum, and urethra. Any activity that puts high-risk bodily fluids into contact with open cuts or any of these mucous membranes is an activity that carries the risk of HIV transmission.

Vaginal Intercourse

During vaginal intercourse, a male penis enters a female vagina and ejaculates upon orgasm. If the man is HIV-positive, the virus will be projected into the woman's vagina, where it can easily be absorbed by the mucous membrane lining the vagina, the largest area of exposure during intercourse.[5] Females, the receiving partners of vaginal intercourse, carry a much higher risk of exposure than males because the vagina serves as a receptacle for potentially infected fluids. Males also have a window of exposure, however, though it is much smaller. The tip of the penis houses the urethra, the canal from which urine and semen are discharged. As mentioned above, the urethra is lined with mucous membrane, so infected blood or vaginal fluids entering the penis's tip could transmit the virus.

Microscopic or even larger cuts can also occur to the genital areas of either partner during vaginal intercourse, due to the friction of skin on skin. Because these cuts can be so small, neither partner may be aware that they have occurred. Whether the participants are aware of them or not, however, the cuts provide direct access for the virus to enter an unsuspecting partner's bloodstream or to leave an infected partner and jeopardize the companion's uninfected mucous membranes. Cuts or tears on the penis can also occur as a result of masturbation, so the penis may have openings to the bloodstream even before entering the vagina.

Anal Intercourse

Anal intercourse is the most dangerous of all sexual activities for HIV transmission. As we have discussed previously, anal intercourse can occur between a male and a female or between two males. Just as is the vagina, the rectum is lined with mucous membranes that absorb blood, semen, and HIV. Also like the vagina, the rectum is the receptacle for the possibly HIV-infected fluids. When a penis ejaculates into a rectum, the semen will be absorbed into the mucous membrane, which is thinner than in the vagina and allows easier absorption. Any STDs that accompany the sperm, including HIV, will be absorbed as well.[6] Another difference that makes the rectum a more dangerous receptacle than the vagina is that the anus is a smaller

orifice and the rectum is a narrower, tighter canal. Forcing a penis
into the more constricted passage is much more likely to result in
tears and cuts to both the penis and the rectum. Further, a large
number of tiny blood vessels lie just below the rectum's surface and
can easily be ruptured, thus providing direct access to the bloodstream and the same opportunities for HIV transmission as discussed
above.

Oral Sex

Likewise, oral sex offers a similar set of risks when blood, semen, or
vaginal fluids are involved. One difference, which might explain
why fewer cases of HIV transmission have been attributed to oral sex
than to vaginal or anal sex, is a recently identified enzyme in saliva
that keeps HIV from entering cells.[7] While this may make HIV less
likely to be transmitted into the mouth, the theoretical danger of
oral sex continues to come from the mucous membranes that line
the mouth and throat and provide entry points for the virus.
Further, other points of entry in the mouth are also feasible. The
chance for blood being present is higher than one might initially
think. Cold sores or other cuts present open wounds, and blood is
often drawn from the gums during a thorough brushing or flossing
of teeth. Semen, vaginal fluids, and blood all pose a threat in oral
sex. Warnings about oral sex must include not only fellatio and cunnilingus but also a less popular activity, anilingus, or licking the
anus. Gays sometimes refer to this practice as "rimming." Blood-to-
blood transmission is the main threat here.

The admonitions about oral sex beg the question of potential
HIV transmission through open-mouth, or French, kissing. No cases
of HIV transmission through kissing have ever been reported; however, kissing is often followed by even higher-risk activities such as
those described above. Although saliva does not carry HIV in a high
enough concentration to pose a threat, the possibility of blood-to-
blood transmission does exist. Again, cold sores or bleeding around
the teeth after brushing and flossing allow entry and exit points for
the virus to travel to or from the bloodstream. To keep from becoming alarmist, we repeat that HIV transmission through any form of
kissing has never been reported.[8] The theoretical possibility, however, does remain.

The Danger of Preejaculatory Fluid

The list of high-risk bodily fluids above included preejaculatory fluid along with semen. Preejaculatory fluid is present in the penis during an erection and is secreted, as its name suggests, before an ejaculation. HIV is present in this fluid, as is sperm in some cases.[9] One method of protection against pregnancy during intercourse has historically been "pulling out," in which the man removes his penis from the vagina before ejaculation. As a guard against HIV, this technique has also been extended to anal and oral intercourse. Unfortunately, because HIV and sometimes sperm are present in preejaculatory fluid, both HIV infection and pregnancy remain possible, even if ejaculation does not occur. Because of this threat, condoms should be put in place well before ejaculation.

Is Protection a Possibility?

Protection against each of these forms of transmission is possible, of course. The first and surest method of protecting against HIV infection is abstinence. If these fluids never have a chance of entering the body, then obviously they cannot and will not. If students can be convinced to abstain from any sexual activity, they will be virtually immune to sexual transmission of the virus. Even if they stop to think about the risk more often and practice any of these sexual activities less often, they will lower their risk.

As any realistic teacher knows, however, many students will continue to engage in sexual activity. Although they cannot receive complete protection, as they can through abstinence, sexually active students can considerably lower their risk through the use of condoms.

Latex condoms, when used properly, provide a barrier between HIV and the bloodstream of an uninfected person. HIV, whether in blood, semen, or vaginal fluids, cannot pass through the sheath of latex to come into contact with blood or mucous membranes. Condoms made from natural membrane, such as lambskin, are not impervious to the virus. Because they are made from animal skin, natural membrane condoms have pores through which HIV can pass. The pores are not large enough to allow sperm to pass through, so this type of condom remains an effective contraceptive. To protect against HIV infection properly, condoms must be used in every sexual situation that involves an erect penis: vaginal intercourse, anal intercourse, and fellatio. A latex condom on a penis can keep the virus either inside or outside, as is necessary.

As we all know, condoms are not completely effective in preventing either HIV infection or pregnancy. However, in most cases, the failure is the responsibility of the user and not the condom. Condoms are tested for breakage and leakage by the manufacturers, the Food and Drug Administration (FDA), and other agencies. According to Dr. Stephen Satcher, director of the CDC, "the average batch tests better than 99.7% defect-free."[10] This number translates to fewer than three defective condoms per one thousand. If a batch of condoms does not perform up to a certain standard, the entire batch is discarded. When students are trained to use condoms correctly and safely, then their risk of condom failure should run well below one percent.

If most condom failure is the result of human error in the use of condoms, then teachers should include some material in their curriculum on the proper use of condoms. Traditionally, this has been information passed by word of mouth from one teen to another. The probability of some misinformation being included along the grapevine is very likely. Because males do not usually embrace the idea of using condoms in the first place, they have had very little reason to research the subject to make sure that their understanding of condoms is correct. Some teachers may find this material somewhat distasteful, but if students do not hear it here, they will likely not hear an "official" version anywhere.

A fresh condom is necessary for each new act of intercourse. Some people try to reuse their condoms, but after a condom has been stretched over an erect penis, it should never be used again, even if the male did not ejaculate into it. The condom package should be opened by carefully tearing down one edge. Individuals trying to rip into it down the middle risk tearing the condom itself. After the package is open, the condom should be removed carefully, by squeezing the bottom and forcing the condom to come out of the end. Grabbing the condom and forcefully pulling it out of the package can also cause damage. Condoms are damaged if they have torn slightly or even been simply pricked. If blood or semen can seep out or vaginal fluid in, the condom is of no use. The damage to a condom does not need to be obvious or noticed at all for the condom to be compromised. The condom can be snagged on a sharp fingernail or a point on a ring setting.

An unused condom is rolled almost flat. A small reservoir is visible in the middle of the rolled condom. This becomes the tip when the condom is unrolled and is intended to hold the ejaculate after the male reaches orgasm. Again being careful of fingernails, the condom user should gently grasp the tip to push the air out. Still grasping the tip, the condom user should place the rolled condom over the head of the erect penis and begin unrolling it. Teens should be warned not to try to place a condom on an unerect penis. Condoms are very similar to balloons, and when used properly they are likewise airtight. If the penis is not erect when a condom is placed on it, it will probably not be big enough to make the condom airtight. A condom that is not airtight, obviously, will leak, undermining the entire purpose of using the condom in the first place. Adding further risk to the situation, as the penis becomes erect, it will stretch the condom unevenly and make breakage a distinct possibility. Rolled condoms have a definite top and bottom and will only unroll one way. If the condom is placed upside down on the penis, it will be difficult to unroll, and persistent attempts to unroll it anyway will only cause damage. A condom placed right side up on the penis will unroll very easily. It should be unrolled to its entire length.

After ejaculation, the condom should be removed from the penis before the penis has a chance to contract, because the condom will not shrink back to its original size. If the couple waits too long to remove the condom, the penis will get smaller, and the airtight bond that had been established around the condom will be broken. Once the condom is no longer airtight, semen can easily leak out. The condom should be removed very carefully to avoid spilling any of the semen inside it. The condom obviously cannot be rolled up again and must be pulled off. Pulling a condom off the penis by the tip may result in breakage, and will almost certainly cause spillage. The condom's rim at the base of the penis should be held so that nothing is spilled.

Once the condom is removed, it should be disposed of immediately. The most obvious receptacle for the condom is the toilet, but not all sexual activity takes place in close proximity to a bathroom. If it is placed in a trash can or other type of waste container, the user should make sure that the container is secure and that there is no chance that someone else might be able to come across the used condom. Both partners must continue to be careful after the condom has been removed. The semen contained in it still has the capability of impregnating a female or, if it is HIV-positive, infecting the partner. Likewise, some semen will remain on the penis after the condom has been taken off, so care should be taken that the penis does not come into contact with the vagina or any easily infected area.

One of the complaints males most often make about condoms is that they diminish the physical sensations of the penis. Some females find condoms uncomfortable as well. One simple method of addressing these problems is to use lubricants along with the condom. Lubricants can make condoms more comfortable and add another element of safety as well. Some brands of condoms come with lubrication, but many do not. If any lubrication is added by the participants, it must be a water-based lubricant, such as K-Y jelly. Oil-based lubricants, such as baby oil, vaseline, vegetable oil, or olive oil, can break down the latex in the condom, ultimately causing it to dissolve. Some condom failure has been attributed to the use of oil-based lubricants. Sexual partners who are carefully making sure to use the condom correctly can negate their efforts with the choice of an oil-based lubricant.

Condoms must not only be used carefully, they must be stored carefully as well. Condoms should never be taken out of their packages until they are ready to be used. If they are unwrapped, they have nothing to protect them from damage. Contrary to popular practice, people should not carry condoms in their wallets or back pockets. In those locations, the condoms will be exposed to the sharp edges of coins and keys, and will continuously be pinched and squashed as people sit on them time after time. By the time such a condom is removed from its wrapper, it will very likely already be damaged. Likewise, condoms should not be stored in a location where they are exposed to heat or direct light. As with balloons, these elements can stretch and weaken the condom. A recent development in condom packaging is for condom manufacturers to acknowledge that condoms do not age well. Most condom packages carry an expiration date. Any condoms not used by this date should be disposed of rather than used because the latex may have begun to decay and is likely to break during use.

Condoms should always be used in conjunction with spermicides. As the name suggests, spermicides kill sperm in order to prevent pregnancy. Many spermicides, particularly those containing nonoxynol-9, have been found to kill HIV as well. Because it is unlikely that the application of spermicide can completely cover an area of potential transmission without some sort of barrier to limit the movement of the virus, spermicides are not considered reliable enough to allow effective protection by themselves. They do, however, provide an effective backup to condoms.[11] If for any reason the condom does fail during sexual activity, a spermicide will likely kill whatever virus may be present. Some condoms come with a spermicide, most often included in the lubrication. Condoms with spermicide obviously offer more convenience than adding a spermicide later. If students buy the condom with spermicide, they will not have to worry about making a separate purchase of spermicide as well.

Other forms of contraception will not double as protection against HIV or other STDs. Birth control pills, obviously, offer no barrier and thus no security against the virus. A diaphragm does offer a barricade in front of the cervix to keep sperm from fertilizing eggs, but offers nothing to prevent HIV from coming into contact with the mucous membrane in the vagina. Spermicides are usually used with a diaphragm, but as we have just discussed, they will not offer enough protection by themselves. Spermicidal sponges and IUDs do not form any sort of barrier and can do nothing to prevent HIV transmission. Finally, natural contraception, or the rhythm method, uses no outside materials at all, and provides absolutely no protection against the transmission of HIV or STDs. Although most of these methods can protect a woman from becoming pregnant, they do nothing at all to keep either partner safe from infection by HIV.

Latex condoms are useful when an erect penis is involved, but some forms of oral sex do not require a penis. In the cases of cunnilingus or anilingus, a penis is not involved. Protected participation in these activities is still possible, however, with the use of a dental dam, a thin, square sheet of latex commonly used by dentists while working on teeth. A dental dam should be spread over the vagina or anus before oral sex occurs in order to prevent the exchange of any fluids. Dental dams used by dentists have a hole in the middle so that the dentist can work on teeth, and thus they will not offer proper protection. Dental dams for sexual protection are available in some stores, but if they are not, they can easily be replicated with a latex condom. The top and bottom of an unrolled, unused condom can be cut off, and a slit cut down one side. When spread out, the condom provides a latex sheet similar to a dental dam, and can serve the same purpose. If neither a dental dam nor a condom are available, plastic wrap for food can provide an effective substitute. If any of these materials becomes punctured during oral sex, the activity should be stopped immediately and the protective barrier replaced.

HOW IS HIV TRANSMITTED AMONG IV DRUG USERS?

Sharing needles for intravenous drug use provides an even more effective method of transmitting HIV than sexual activity. During various sexual encounters with an HIV-positive partner, the virus is exposed to areas of the body into which it can be absorbed. Intravenous drug use, however, involves the shooting of substances directly into the bloodstream. The equipment, or "works," for IV drugs include needles, syringes, and containers from which the drugs are drawn into the syringe, such as bottle caps, spoons, or cotton balls. When these works are used to inject drugs, they inevitably come into contact with blood. Many users employ techniques that bring blood into the syringe, such as pulling the plunger back to make sure the needle has hit a vein. Even if the syringe appears to be empty before it is passed to the next user, blood can remain in trace amounts on the side of the syringe, in the cavity of the needle, or around the rubber stopper. When this syringe is passed on to the next user, he or she is guaranteed to inject some of the first user's blood directly into the bloodstream. If the first user is HIV positive, the results of this action are obvious. HIV, in a large enough concentration for infection, is forced into the bloodstream, and virtually guarantees an HIV-positive blood test for the user sometime in the future.

Piercing and Tattoo Needles

Although most adolescents do not take part in such activity, the threat of HIV transmission through needles is real for them. The same ingredients that make sharing drug needles dangerous can be extended to sharing needles or any other implements used for body piercing or tattoos. As with drug use, the needle itself is not threatening; it is only the blood that may remain on the needle that poses a problem. In the past, ears were commonly the only part of the body to be pierced, and many young girls continue this practice in informal gatherings. If this activity, even among elementary school students, involves sharing needles, it is a risk activity for HIV infection. More and more, however, virtually every part of the body has become a potential site for piercing. Tattoos, both professional and amateur, have also recently returned to vogue. A needle used on one person for either piercing or tattoos will retain traces of that person's blood, which can then be placed into the next person's body if the needle is used again. Amateur piercing or tattooing at home, as well as professional piercing or tattooing in unsanitary conditions, presents a threat. The same needle should never be used on more than one person unless it has been thoroughly cleaned. A reused piercing or tattoo needle presents an optimum circumstance for passing the virus on.

Reaching IV Drug Users

As we can see, sharing needles and "works" to inject IV drugs is a much more efficient method of transmitting HIV than sexual activity. Why, then, has an effort equal to that for preventing sexual transmission not been mounted to address IV drug users? For the most part, IV drug use has its own subculture that does not interact with the greater mainstream culture to any great degree. Fewer people inject drugs than have sex, obviously, so transmission through IV drug use is not as large a threat to the greater population as is transmission through sexual activity. Sexual partners of IV drug users are at risk for HIV infection, but the virus generally stays within the same small circle. IV drug use among junior high and high school students has not been reported in large quantities, so less class time is usually assigned to this information. Adolescents who inject IV drugs have usually already dropped out of school, and are thus no longer able to hear the preventive message. This makes an excellent argument for introducing AIDS education, particularly material about IV drug use, in late elementary school or middle school. Students at risk for dropping out and taking part in high-risk behavior as teenagers will still be under the influence of the school system and may hear this vital information that can later save their lives.

Can IV Drugs Be Injected Safely?

The risk of becoming infected with HIV by sharing needles can be completely eliminated by never injecting IV drugs or getting a tattoo or a piercing. Of course, just as with sex, some students are not going to choose to abstain from these activities. The second line of defense against transmitting the virus through needles is for the IV drug user to be very sure never to share needles or works with anyone else. If no one else's blood is allowed to make contact with either the needle or the works, infected blood cannot be injected into the user's bloodstream. While under the influence, unfortunately, IV drug users often do not have the presence of mind to make sure no one else uses their works, or even necessarily to differentiate their works from anyone else's. In such cases, they must fall back on the third line of defense against HIV, cleaning their works.

AIDS has taken the scientific and medical communities by surprise, and resources for research and prevention have been very limited. Doctors and other scientists have had to set priorities in investigating how the virus affects the body and ways in which it can be treated effectively. Their priorities have not included determining how IV drug users can clean their works in order to inject drugs without the threat of HIV infection. Little scientific research has been conducted on this subject. However, through trial and error, some general guidelines have been established. Like using a condom during sexual intercourse, methods of cleaning needles and works are not one hundred percent foolproof. Errors made when cleaning the works, as well as possible errors in the method of cleaning itself, can occur and can allow the virus to be transmitted from one IV drug user to another. The latest thinking on needle cleaning is first to use warm water to rinse the syringe and needle twice immediately after shooting up. The warm water should be poured into the syringe and then squirted out into a waste receptacle such as a sink or toilet bowl. The water should not be returned to the container from which it came and from which new water will be drawn, because any HIV in the syringe will infect the water, and the syringe will not be clean. Next, pour bleach into the syringe and tap it for about thirty seconds. This process should be completed twice. The bleach should disinfect the syringe, stopper, plunger, and needle. Finally, the syringe should be rinsed with water several more times. This final act might seem unimportant because the syringe should already be disinfected. It is necessary, however, in order to make sure that all the bleach has been rinsed out of the syringe. Injecting bleach into the bloodstream is also dangerous for IV drug users.

ARE THERE ANY OTHER WAYS HIV CAN BE TRANSMITTED?

Another method of HIV transmission, but one that likely will not concern many adolescents, is transmission from a mother to a baby. If a pregnant woman is infected with HIV, she can pass the virus on to her baby in the womb or during the birthing process. Transmission in the womb is not a given, however, and it is more than likely that an HIV-positive mother will give birth to an HIV-negative baby. Recent research suggests that only twenty to twenty-five percent of babies born to HIV-positive mothers will be infected with the virus. The father's HIV status is completely irrelevant. While a man can transmit the virus to a woman through intercourse, because HIV is found in the fluid surrounding sperm but not in the sperm itself he cannot infect the child conceived during that intercourse.[12] If the HIV-positive mother breast-feeds the baby, however, she can also transmit the virus through her breast milk.

When AIDS first began to be noticed by doctors, before it had even been given the name AIDS, some people were infected with HIV through blood transfusions. Also, a large percentage of hemophiliacs became infected through tainted blood products prescribed for their disease. When HIV was identified as the cause of AIDS and was found to exist in blood, health officials set out to seek and destroy all tainted blood in the nation's blood supply. Blood products for hemophiliacs were also heat disinfected. This occurred in 1985. Since that time, all donated blood has been tested for the virus and has been destroyed if the virus has been found. Organs available for transplant also go through a rigorous testing process to insure that they are free of HIV. The nation's blood supply is not overtly threatened by HIV. Still, because new blood is introduced into the body during a blood transfusion, it remains theoretically possible to become infected. If an infected person donates blood during the small window of time between infection and detection, tainted blood can enter the health system. Health professionals estimate that the chances of HIV-infected blood being used in a transfusion is less than 5 in 100,000 cases.[13] Given the other dangers that a patient faces during an operation in which a blood transfusion is necessary, the threat of HIV infection is a minor worry, indeed.

WHAT ARE THE COMMON MYTHS OF HIV TRANSMISSION?

Earlier in this chapter we stated that HIV is both easy and difficult to transmit. So far we have discussed the conditions and circumstances that make HIV easy to transmit. Now we will examine what makes it difficult for HIV to pass from person to person, and why many of those most concerned with contracting the virus need not be. The first scientific fact that keeps HIV and AIDS from being an even larger threat is that HIV can thrive only in bodily fluids. Although it does not necessarily die immediately upon exposure to outside air, HIV cannot exist in a large or strong enough concentration to be infectious.[14] Other viruses, such as the flu, can thrive and multiply in the air, which makes them able to be passed from one person to another by coughing, sneezing, or just breathing the same air. It is only natural for some students to fear that they can be infected by HIV in the same way.

Casual Contact

As we discussed earlier, although HIV is present in a number of bodily fluids, it is only concentrated enough to infect others in the four that make up the *high-risk bodily fluids*: blood, semen (including pree-jaculatory fluid), vaginal fluids, and breast milk. Other bodily fluids, such as saliva, sweat, tears, or urine, some of which are more likely than the four high-risk fluids to come into casual contact with other people, carry no HIV at all or only trace amounts. If a student were to come into contact with the saliva, sweat, tears, or urine of an HIV-infected person, the student would have absolutely no known risk of becoming infected with the virus. These fluids can carry other germs and viruses, however, so contact with them is not always free of any potential infection. Urine, as the waste of the human body, can particularly carry unhealthy ingredients that can cause illness to others. Any people who do come into contact with these bodily fluids should thoroughly wash their hands and any skin surfaces that have touched the fluid.

Because HIV cannot survive outside human bodily fluids, it can also not be transmitted through touching or other such contact. HIV will not survive in food, drinks, or on surfaces such as water fountains or toilet seats. Again, because there are other viruses that can be transmitted from one person to another by eating from the same plate or utensils, drinking from the same glass, or touching the same surfaces as an infected person, the fear of HIV being contagious in the same manner is understandable. HIV cannot be transmitted so easily. Many people have lived for a number of years in the same house as an HIV-positive family member, and there has never been a report of the virus being transmitted through such casual methods.[15]

Students need have no fear of being infected by an HIV-infected family member or friend with whom they spend time or share various materials. Likewise, they should have no reason to feel threatened if an HIV-positive student joins their class at school.

Mosquito Bites

Another common misperception of HIV transmission is the idea that it can be transmitted through mosquito bites. Like other myths about AIDS, this one sounds possible. Some diseases, such as malaria, can be transmitted from one person to another by mosquitos, so this fear is rational. Adding to the fear of mosquito bites is the fact that mosquitos draw blood when they bite people, and HIV is a blood-borne virus. Although both these facts are true, the key word to remember is the first word in HIV, *human*. HIV is a virus of humans, and it will not survive in mosquitos. Even if a mosquito bites someone who is HIV-positive, the virus cannot be passed on to the next person bitten by the mosquito because the virus will not live long enough. Also, it must be noted that mosquitos only *withdraw* blood. They do not inject blood from past bite victims into new bite victims.[16] HIV will not exist outside humans, so mosquitos, or any other animals for that matter, cannot be carriers.

Infection from Health Care Workers

A number of myths related to the health care field have demonstrated quite a bit of staying power. Many people know that HIV is present in human blood, so the idea that HIV can infect a person who donates blood or can be transmitted by health care workers has refused to die. Both are untrue. When someone donates blood, the health care worker taking the blood uses entirely new equipment— new needles, new syringes, new tubing—and disposes of that equipment after each person gives blood. HIV can only be spread by sharing blood, and with all-new equipment, there is no blood to share.

Likewise, health care personnel take extreme care when handling blood. They do not want to become infected themselves if one of their patients is HIV-positive, and the precautions they take, disposing of or rigorously cleaning any materials that come into contact with blood, will prevent them from passing the virus to any patients. There have been no definitely proven cases of any health care worker—doctor, nurse, dentist, or any other—infecting any of their patients with HIV.

Casual contact has so far never been shown to be a cause of HIV transmission. HIV is difficult to get because one must engage in very particular behaviors that allow the virus access to the bloodstream. Students can be set at ease with this information, and any students who are currently sexually active can hear the warning to protect themselves. We certainly know by now, however, that students are quite unlikely to take this information by itself and act upon it, so the following chapters address techniques that educators can use to influence their students' attitudes and behaviors more effectively.

4

Age-Appropriate Information

It appears that as children age and their concepts of the world develop, their understanding of illness changes to match that conceptualization. Young children do not make a distinction among different types or severities of illnesses, but develop their understanding of all illness in the same way. Therefore, whatever a young child can understand about the common cold, he or she can understand about AIDS. Students should be taught as much about AIDS as they are prepared to understand. AIDS education, then, should be keyed to children's level of development. Young children have a very low ability to understand disease and illness, and so should not be saddled with terminology and details that will mean nothing to them. Older children and teenagers, with a progressively larger ability to conceptualize disease, should be given as much information about AIDS as they can comprehend. Just as is true in all educational endeavors, the outside edge of students' understanding should always be challenged.

APPROPRIATE AGE TO BEGIN AIDS INSTRUCTION

A great deal of worry and contention has surrounded the question of at what age AIDS education should first be introduced to students. One group of parents polled divided themselves into three fairly equal camps on the issue, with one third desiring education as early as six or seven years old, another third preferring eight or nine years old, and a final third advocating ten or eleven years old. Teachers and educators are also split on the question. In separate surveys of teachers and superintendents, the percentage of educators who believed that AIDS education should begin by third grade fell between twenty and twenty-five percent. Fifty-four percent of the teachers felt that it should be in place no later than fifth grade, but only thirty-nine percent of superintendents agreed. A little more than a third of superintendents thought that AIDS education could be held off until middle school.[1]

While it is easy to understand the reluctance of educators to plunge into such a controversial subject matter as AIDS, none of these ages is early enough for AIDS education to begin. Children are ready to learn about HIV and AIDS as soon as they are old enough to come across the subject on their own, overhearing a parental conversation or a report on television news. Many preschoolers or kindergartners have already encountered these terms in a context of unease and fear. If for no other reason than to put their young minds at ease concerning HIV as a potential threat to them, the subject of HIV and AIDS should be presented to them in school. Some sort of AIDS education should be initiated as early as kindergarten. If teachers determine that their younger preschoolers already have an awareness or concern about AIDS, they should introduce their classes to the subject as well.

YOUNG CHILDREN

AIDS education can perform at its most perfunctory level for young children ranging from kindergarten to third grade. Children in these grades are at very low risk for encountering HIV and at virtually no risk for becoming infected by it. They need to know very few details about the virus or the disease, and likely would not understand any but the most basic. Still, AIDS has most likely permeated their awareness and must, therefore, be addressed in some way. In two different studies, approximately two-thirds of first graders were familiar with AIDS. They knew the word and had made their own connotations with it. Of those who recognized the term, more than a third expected that they or someone they knew would contract AIDS.[2] This worry probably comes from concern that people can become infected with HIV through casual contact with an infected person, such as touching or being too close to someone with HIV.

Based on these misconceptions, young children may develop a number of questions, such as: What is AIDS? Does everyone who gets AIDS die? and Will I get AIDS? For the most part, these questions and others like them can be answered by using quite simple concepts and terms. To explain AIDS or HIV to children in too much detail needlessly complicates matters. Before the age of six or seven, children do not comprehend how illness works. They may know the proper terminology of disease, such as "virus," "germ," and "infection," but the words mean little if anything to them. Teachers have to make sure that they are not fooled into believing that simply because children can parrot back the correct terms they have any idea what those terms mean. If teachers ask their students to explain AIDS, they might end up with such responses as: "AIDS is when you get sick." Following that with a request for students to explain how HIV causes AIDS might elicit only: "It just does." Understanding, not correct repetition of the right words, should be the focus of AIDS education. The ideas of sexual activity or drug abuse are even more complex, and are virtually unfathomable to young children. As far as most children of this age are concerned, sickness might as well be caused by magic.

Content

The main concern teachers of this age group should have in regard to AIDS education is to allay any fears their students may have about AIDS. In fact, the Centers for Disease Control addresses only the alleviation of fear in its guidelines for this age. According to the CDC, students should be told that AIDS has made some adults very sick, but that children do not easily come into contact with the disease. Further, AIDS is very difficult to get, and cannot be transmitted by touching or being close to someone who has it. As a final reassurance, the CDC suggests that students be told about scientists all over the world working for an end to the disease.[3] In broad terms, this is probably all that teachers of younger children need worry about conveying to their students. More specifically, in light of children's worries about their own vulnerability, teachers can identify safe behaviors and undermine myths about AIDS transmission by explaining that mosquitos do not carry HIV, people cannot get HIV from a toilet seat or by forgetting to wash their hands, and that HIV cannot be spread by sitting next to an infected person. Younger children are likely not yet old enough to understand how HIV does spread, so little or no time should be built into the curriculum to try to cover that.

Because teachers are trying to assuage worry and concern, it is important that they allow time for student questions and discussion. Children should be given time to state their fears and their ideas about AIDS. Many parents, who may harbor their own concerns about HIV and AIDS, have not spent a lot of time talking with their children or soothing fears about the subject, so the classroom may be the only opportunity students get to share plain talk about AIDS. Some teachers may feel awkward allowing their young students to share what may be uninformed views, but the openness of classroom dialogue will encourage the students to feel that their ideas are worth talking about, and will stimulate them to share their feelings in other forums. Any misinformation can quickly and easily be corrected by the teacher. As was discussed earlier, talking specifically about HIV and AIDS will let children know that they are welcomed and encouraged to communicate about what is too often a closed topic in our society.

In introducing any of this material, teachers should keep in mind that children of this age mostly relate everything they learn to themselves and their individual experience. Any discussion of sickness will be thought of in terms of sick relatives or friends. Some children will have grandparents or great-grandparents who have become sick and have died. They will worry that the subject of illness automatically equates to the subject of death. Instead of trying to tiptoe around that subject, teachers have an excellent opportunity to differentiate between some diseases that often end in death and some that do not. Children who have some experience with death may worry that any sniffle or cough they or their parents develop will lead inevitably to death. Young children are only beginning to learn how to sort through information, and teachers can use this occasion to help students break down their understanding of illnesses to differentiate between fatal and nonfatal diseases. If teachers feel that their students have a high enough level of sophistication, they may want to introduce the idea that all sicknesses are not the same. Different types of sicknesses, they might teach, have different kinds of causes, different kinds of symptoms, and different kinds of treatments. Students may have had personal experience with chicken pox or the flu, which in modern times are not generally life-threatening illnesses and which also do not each have the same symptoms. These or other sicknesses might provide teachers with excellent examples of how illnesses can differ in their effects and outcomes. If, however, students do not seem to respond to the information, it may be beyond their conceptual abilities at that time. As always, teachers should reach their own judgment of the appropriate material for their classes.

OLDER CHILDREN

As children get older, reaching fourth grade and into middle school, there is no question that they are aware of the concepts of HIV and AIDS. Although they probably know very little correct and concrete information on the subject, they likely believe that they do. Just as more of these students are familiar with HIV and AIDS, they are more concerned with the effects AIDS might have on them personally. In a survey of fifth graders, almost half of the students believed that they or someone they know will contract AIDS.[4] Fifth graders have a better idea than first graders of the consequences of becoming sick with AIDS, and so the lowering of anxiety is an important component of the curriculum for this age group as well.

Although most older children have not engaged in risky behavior and are at extremely low vulnerability for HIV infection, some of them are not very far from becoming sexually active, and a few have already experienced their sexual initiation. Because of this, classes in late elementary school probably offer the greatest range of experiences within the same class for a teacher to consider. Some children who are not yet sexually experienced will be sexually knowledgeable, and some will have very little awareness of sexuality on any conscious level. Teachers will have to prepare their educational program on a class-by-class basis, trying their best to determine the level of information and skills necessary for each class. Unfortunately, as we have already seen, those children most at risk have the lowest level of anxiety concerning HIV infection. AIDS instructors, then, will be called upon to lower the anxiety level of those not at risk while stimulating an appropriate level of anxiety for those who do practice risky behaviors.

The level of understanding has also risen in these children, of course, and much more detail about HIV and AIDS can be successfully broached than could with younger children. Older children have reached a level of development in which they can see that a concrete world exists outside themselves. This understanding does not go very far beyond things that the children can see and touch, however, and abstract ideas and theories are almost completely beyond them. The concept of an external agent, HIV, entering the body and causing AIDS does make sense to them, and so specific risky and nonrisky behaviors can be described. Myths about HIV transmission can be attacked on a logical level, and teachers need not worry that their students must merely accept the material on faith. More abstract ideas, however, such as the difference between a virus and a bacterium or the way in which a virus enters the bloodstream and attacks the immune system, are still beyond them. Students at this age may or may not be able to differentiate between HIV and AIDS, and may refer to both the infecting agent and the disease as AIDS. Teachers might make initial attempts to distinguish the two concepts, but if students do not quickly make the distinction themselves, there is no reason to press the issue. Little harm is caused by fourth or fifth graders combining the two ideas into one.

Students at this age are likely to ask more penetrating questions about AIDS than their younger counterparts. They will want to know more about specific methods of HIV transmission or nontransmission, such as holding hands, hugging, and perhaps even sexual intercourse. Questions about how we can tell if someone has HIV or AIDS are likely to be raised. A few students may even wonder why, if having sex is dangerous because of HIV infection, people do not simply stop having sex. This, of course, is a very difficult question to answer. Many older children, not yet reaching puberty, have little idea of the power of the sex drive. Teachers can use this question as a jumping off point for describing protective measures for sexual activity that allow sex to be safer. When addressing actual sexual desire, which may be unfathomable to some students, teachers will have to describe the emotions and yearnings of the sex drive in whatever way they feel most comfortable. Since young children often are aware of the sex drive and pleasure through masturbation, this could be one way to illuminate it.

Children in later elementary school are also likely to ask questions about HIV transmission based on convoluted scenarios. "What if it was raining on an HIV-positive woman and then she dripped on me?" "What if an HIV-positive man who had a cut in his mouth gave me a kiss?" "What if someone got HIV in a water fountain before I took a drink out of it?" Most of these questions will be quite easy to answer for the teacher who is well grounded in the facts of AIDS. HIV cannot be transferred through raindrops. HIV can be transmitted through blood in the mouth, but the person receiving the kiss would also have to have a cut in order for HIV to enter his or her body, and the amount of blood necessary would be noticeable. Besides, who would want to kiss anyone with a visible cut in their mouth in the first place? HIV cannot exist on an outside surface like a water fountain. Students may try to trip teachers up, thinking of loopholes in the facts, but teachers who keep their wits about them and use common sense will be able to keep everything set straight.

Content

Older children are prepared to accept and work through more factual information about HIV and AIDS than they had been in earlier grades. Although teachers should still give enough attention to helping students develop an accurate perception of their individual risk, they can also spend time on AIDS facts and skill development. The CDC suggests that AIDS education at this level consist primarily of factual information. Older children will be able to understand the concept of viruses as microscopic organisms which enter the body and cause illness. They can be told that different viruses have different effects on people. HIV, of course, is a virus, but so is the flu, which causes fever, chills, aches, and pains. A stomach virus can cause nausea and vomiting. HIV causes damage to the body's immune system, which helps it fight off other viruses or diseases. Students should also be told that sometimes a virus, as in the case of HIV, can take a long time to start working. No one can tell who carries a virus and who does not, so students should not expect to be able to know whether or not someone has a virus by looking at them.[5]

After the connection between AIDS and the immune system is established, the CDC guidelines continue, teachers should list and explain common AIDS-related illnesses such as Kaposi's sarcoma (KS) and pneumocystis carinii pneumonia (PCP). The social aspects of AIDS should not be left out and, according to the CDC, teachers should explain that people infected with HIV have been found in every one of the fifty states and in most other countries. People in every walk of life and all types of communities, cities, small towns, suburbs, and rural areas have proven to be vulnerable to AIDS. Although adults make up the majority of HIV infections, HIV-positive people of all ages can be found. HIV-positive individuals have included men and women, whites, African Americans, Asians, Native Americans, and Hispanics. Teachers should let students see the full extent of the AIDS pandemic by providing the most recent statistics they can find about the estimated number of people infected with HIV in this country and in the rest of the world, as well as the total number of AIDS fatalities at home and abroad, and the estimated number of current AIDS cases.[6]

The CDC guidelines suggest that HIV transmission be discussed in general terms, but many teachers will find it appropriate to specifically identify methods in which HIV can be transmitted from one person to another: sexual contact with someone who is infected, sharing needles with someone who is infected, from infected mother to infant. In addition, teachers should also be prepared to identify the four fluids that transmit HIV. If they are not addressed in the classroom, it is certain they will be addressed in hushed tones, wrapped in suggestion, innuendo, and misinformation, in the parking lot or on the playground. Although these students may not yet have the level of understanding necessary to describe how HIV affects the body, they will understand that it is an external agent that must be kept outside the body. At this age, that is enough to know. Teachers can offer information about how HIV might enter the body, and students can learn the appropriate protections. Except for blood, however, each of these fluids has sexual connotations, and teachers will need to determine the level of detail they should deal with for each class. Some teachers will feel that their students have enough knowledge and awareness of sexuality that they can discuss these issues explicitly. In fact, some teachers of students as young as fifth grade may have seen one or two of their students become pregnant during the school year. Surely such students, already practicing AIDS-risk behavior, must address routes of transmission in detail.

A group of educators in the Midwest developed a pilot program of AIDS education for fifth and sixth graders based closely on the CDC guidelines. The intervention, a twenty-five minute slide presentation, was opened to questioning by students throughout, making the presentation about forty-five minutes in all. While developing the program, the educators took note of the area's history of fifth and sixth grade pregnancy, and decided to go beyond the guidelines by adding the topic of latex condoms. During the presentations, the fifth and sixth graders posed a number of questions about French kissing.[7] Teachers are left to their own judgment concerning their particular students and what they need to hear about this topic.

Finishing up the CDC education guidelines for older children are instructions to tell students that some doctors and other medical workers have been infected with HIV after exposure to HIV-positive blood. Although they later point out that donating blood is not a risk activity, the guidelines make no mention of blood transfusions or relieve any worry that, if doctors have been infected, patients might be just as susceptible. Finally, the guidelines indicate that teachers should cover some of the basic medical realities of HIV infection. Symptoms of AIDS-related diseases sometimes do not appear for a number of years after initial infection, so it is impossible to tell if someone is HIV positive simply by looking at them. Not only might an HIV-positive person not look sick, he or she may not even feel sick.[8]

Teachers might be advised to preempt some confusion and concern on the part of their students by spending more time on the subject of medical workers infected through blood contact. This raises two points of concern that students are likely to notice: the threat of infection from blood transfusions, and the threat from doctors, nurses, or dentists. Teachers can return to the previous discussion of these potential concerns.

TEENAGERS

The oldest students, those in high school, provide both the least and the most amount of challenge for teachers. They provide the least amount of challenge in that teachers need expend very little time considering what information is appropriate and what is not. Teenagers have reached a level of understanding about illness and disease that will accept quite sophisticated biological and medical ideas. HIV can be allowed its full explanation as a virus that enters the body and sets about to undermine the T cells that make up the first line of defense in the immune system. Teens can understand that AIDS breaks down the body by lowering the defenses to allow in opportunistic diseases like KS, PCP, and tuberculosis. Teachers do not have to worry about simplifying the material so that their students have a chance of comprehending it. Teens can also understand all the implications of protection and nonprotection. If they do not have actual sexual experience, the vast majority are at least aware of the details of sexual subjects. Teachers can rest assured that there will be very few students in their classes to whom they will have to introduce explicit material for the first time. In terms of preparing the informational material of AIDS education, teenagers definitely provide the least challenge.

Where teenagers become the most difficult challenge to teachers is, in a way, on the flip side of that same ability to understand. Many teenagers have already made up their minds about their behavior and the risk that they believe it involves. They will be harder for teachers to reach and persuade to change their thoughts, attitudes, and actions. Teenagers, in junior high and high school, are likely to ask very probing and difficult questions, such as precisely how HIV is transmitted from man to man or woman to woman, or which sexual actions are relatively safe and which less secure. Teenagers will want specific answers, not some evasive platitudes. They will ask about condom etiquette, wondering if women should carry condoms as well as men, and then they will probe the implications of the teacher's answer.

Teachers will also have the responsibility of helping teenagers gain an accurate perception of their individual level of risk for HIV infection. Those students who have yet to initiate sexual activity and are not in the drug scene will have a very low level of risk, and should be aided in understanding that. Students who do participate in risky sexual or drug behaviors are in danger of HIV infection and should be advised of just that. Unfortunately, as we have noted before, many teachers will be in the dark as to which students fall into which category. Of course, the risk status of some students, good or bad, will appear to be fairly obvious, but the vast majority of students will fall into a gray area of indeterminate risk. And teachers may not always guess correctly about even those students who are apparently conspicuous in their risk or nonrisk. Teachers must maintain a very delicate balance in presenting this material so that each individual student will receive the message he or she needs to hear.

Content

As might be expected, the CDC guidelines are most extensive for teenagers, although they still fall short of the full disclosure one might expect. Medical information can be spelled out in detail for this age group, and teachers should explain what is known about how HIV attacks the body's immune system. Teenagers should be able to comprehend the implications of immune system breakdown and the long delay before symptoms appear. From discussing HIV as an external virus, it is only a quick jump to detailing the modes of transmission through which the virus can enter the body. Before listing these, however, the CDC guidelines make another plea for abstinence. If one does not choose abstinence, the CDC guidelines next address monogamous relationships between noninfected partners, another nonrisk behavior. Only after making clear its position on chastity and faithfulness does the CDC suggest that the various modes of transmission be explained to students. To its credit, the CDC does use specific language to describe risky sexual contact as "penis/vagina, penis/rectum, mouth/vagina, mouth/penis, mouth/rectum" rather than leaving teachers with euphemisms. A bit further down in the guidelines, the possibility of HIV transmission through French kissing is raised. The guidelines correctly point out that no cases of HIV transmission through kissing have ever been documented.[9]

The CDC guidelines go on to mention again that some medical workers have been infected when exposed to HIV-positive blood. Perhaps this point is being raised again as a sort of scare tactic to make teens take the risk of HIV infection seriously. If medical professionals, extensively trained in proper procedure, can become infected, then untrained teenagers should be extra careful. The possibility of patients becoming infected through contact with HIV-positive medical workers remains unaddressed, so teachers will need to set the record straight on this issue. Questions students may raise concerning the risk of infection through a blood transfusion, however, are discussed later in the guidelines for this age group. The CDC makes clear that, although HIV was transmitted to patients undergoing blood transfusions or to hemophiliacs through infected blood clotting products early in the history of AIDS, all blood products and donated blood have been screened and tested for the presence of

HIV since 1985. Hemophiliacs and medical patients in need of transfusions have been at minimum risk for infection since then.[10]

Although AIDS professionals are attempting to avoid the practice of identifying "risk groups" for HIV infection because it carries the risk of scapegoating and personal denial, the CDC does indicate that teenagers increase their own risk of infection by having sexual intercourse with a partner who might be at risk of coming into contact with HIV. This is a tricky issue for teachers. Part of the reason risk groups are no longer identified is that people often refuse to identify themselves with the social tags others may use. Homosexuality is the target of enough social taboos that many people who have had some experience with same-gender sexuality refuse to think of themselves as homosexuals. Indeed, if a person has only one or two same-sex incidents among a large number of opposite-sex experiences, many people might resist identifying him- or herself as homosexual. Therefore, this same person might know that homosexuals are at risk for HIV infection, but by refusing the identification with homosexuality, he or she can also ignore the possibility of exposure to HIV through risky behavior. Instead of falling into this trap of semantics, AIDS professionals have decided to identify risk behaviors rather than risk groups. Whether they consider themselves gay or not, men who have sex with other men are at risk for HIV infection. The CDC guidelines point out that having sex or sharing needles with someone who has likely practiced any or all of these risk behaviors puts one at increased risk for infection.[11] Unfortunately, trying to judge a person's level of risk is a process full of contradictions and circular reasoning. If we do not know a person's history, then we do not know if that is a safe person with whom to become sexually intimate or not. When we do not know, we must act as though everyone is a potential risky partner. Teens are encouraged to assume the worst and treat their potential partner as if they had engaged in risky behaviors.

After all this warning about levels of risk and abstaining or avoiding contact, the CDC guidelines finally broach the subject of protection. For all those teenagers who insist on remaining sexually active, it is suggested that a latex condom "applied properly" will reduce the possible risk. Although there is no indication of how to apply a condom properly, the guidelines advise that a condom should be used from the beginning of the sexual encounter until the end.

After another caveat that condoms do not provide complete protection, the use of spermicides is also recommended. Before forsaking the subject of condoms completely, the guidelines encourage teachers to point out that precautions against HIV protection can also protect against unintended pregnancy and infection by STDs.[12]

The CDC guidelines for material suitable for teenagers begin their final paragraph with an appeal for anyone believing that he or she may be infected with HIV to seek testing. The guidelines correctly point out that testing can establish that an individual is free of HIV infection as well as confirm that such infection exists. If someone tests and is found to be HIV-negative, the results of the test and any counseling that may accompany it will alleviate any anxiety that might be present. Counseling in conjunction with testing can also help people fully understand the seriousness of the AIDS pandemic and the need to continue to practice protective behaviors.[13]

Tests for AIDS can, of course, also confirm the presence of HIV antibodies in the bloodstream. In such a circumstance, counseling should definitely be sought out if it does not accompany the testing. The trauma involved in the realization that one is HIV positive cannot be understated and should not be experienced alone. Counseling can help address the desolation and despair that initially comes with a positive test. According to the CDC guidelines, an individual diagnosed as HIV positive has a number of responsibilities to former, current, and future sexual partners. Current and future sexual partners should be protected from infection through all appropriate methods, including abstinence from insertive sexual activity or the unfailing use of condoms whenever appropriate. An individual should inform current and past partners of his or her newly discovered HIV-positive status so that they can seek the appropriate testing and counseling to determine their own status. Many people who test positive for HIV do not know precisely when they became infected and so cannot limit their warnings only to partners encountered after a particular incident. Although there are no laws requiring disclosure to be made to former sexual partners, ethics demand that anyone in potential danger of being infected be notified.[14]

The CDC also advises HIV-positive females to guard against becoming pregnant and potentially passing the virus to a baby. Although odds are good that a baby born to an HIV-positive mother will not become infected, the possibility remains large enough to be taken seriously.[15]

Finally, the CDC concludes its recommendations for HIV-positive teenagers by advising them to keep very close tabs on their health. AIDS becomes deadly through the opportunistic diseases that take advantage of a weakened immune system to gain a foothold in the body, so careful monitoring and early treatment of any health problems that may develop can help in delaying the effects of AIDS. Medical knowledge and technology are advancing quite rapidly, and someone infected with HIV can, if properly cared for, maintain an active life for more than ten years after the initial infection.[16]

The CDC guidelines do offer some help to the junior high school and high school teacher interested in initiating an AIDS education program, but they certainly overlook a vast wealth of information that may be vital to a number of students. As we have discussed, abstinence, as the only certain method of avoiding HIV infection, is an important part of any AIDS education effort, but it does not tell the whole story. A number of individuals greatly enjoy participating in sex and will continue to do so. If they did not like the experience, they would stop having sex without the threat of AIDS. The human sex drive is an extremely powerful force and will not be denied easily. To discuss protection for sexual activity as grudgingly as these guidelines do is exceptionally unfair to students having sex. Many students are going to have sexual intercourse regardless of what teachers tell them, and they should be able to protect themselves as they do so. Teaching this information may be the difference between experiencing an epidemic of HIV infections among teenagers and not experiencing one. HIV among teens cannot be wiped away entirely, but it can certainly be curtailed, and the only way of doing that is to go beyond the CDC guidelines in presenting protective information. The basic information necessary to a successful program is certainly present within these guidelines, but teachers may need to rethink and reorganize the emphasis given to each element.

Concerned primarily with facts, information, and abstinence, the guidelines give little but lip service to the importance of attitudinal and skills education. By the time they are in high school, some students have begun to express strong homophobic and intolerant attitudes. Teachers will have to do more than simply lay the groundwork for avoiding such attitudes before the fact. In many cases, they will be called upon to face down these attitudes after they have become firmly entrenched in students' belief systems. As discussed earlier, an effective AIDS education instructor will target homophobia and other types of intolerance not just to broaden the minds and attitudes of students, but also to bring down the high level of risk behavior that accompanies such attitudes. Negative attitudes toward things that teens perceive as "causing" AIDS can easily undermine all the positive benefits of AIDS education.

5

Individual and Group Activities
to Uncover the Facts

When the subject matter in a class is as important for students as learning how to protect themselves from HIV infection, a straightforward lecture by the teacher is just not going to have the necessary impact. Teachers need to identify techniques that can help them bring the relevance and significance of HIV infection home to their students. This chapter will outline some activities that teachers may choose to utilize in reaching their students with this vital information. As in Chapter 3, little attempt will be made to assign activities to appropriate age or grade levels. Teachers can pick and choose the activities they feel will be most useful for their individual classes.

GETTING THINGS STARTED

Because a unit of comprehensive AIDS education breaks new ground in at least some areas, teachers and students may both initially be somewhat uncomfortable. It is important, however, to make sure that students are actively engaged in the presentation from the word go.

Ground Rules

To help overcome possible uneasiness or awkwardness, teachers can establish a few ground rules at the beginning of the unit. Student participation is an integral part of the learning process, so students must be put at ease as quickly as possible. These ground rules, in bold type below, can be written out and posted on a bulletin board or wall so that they are in easy sight of everyone.

1 Respect Others. Effective learning is a communal activity. All students in the class must treat each other fairly and respectfully to build the level of trust and openness that is essential to productive AIDS education. Having students ask questions and offer ideas is a vital component of helping this material effect behavior change, and students will not participate to the level they should unless they feel safe from ridicule, derision, and embarrassment.

2 Everything in Our Discussion Should Remain Confidential. This is an extension of the issue of trust and respect. During discussions or other activities in an AIDS information program, personal information is often revealed. Such information offered by students can often be embarrassing or even damaging to themselves or others and should remain in confidence. Teachers may learn information concerning students who face abuse or other danger that might demand some sort of response. This will be discussed later. Students, however, have no reason to discuss sensitive material concerning other students and should not discuss outside the class who said what or who reacted in what way. Often students may ask a question or offer a comment that they later wish they had not. There should be no need for them to worry that a misstatement or misunderstanding will come back to haunt them after being broadcast to the rest of the school.

3 Every Question and Comment Is Helpful. No question or comment should be considered stupid or silly by teachers or other students. All questions should be entertained, and students should be discouraged from laughing at, snickering at, or mocking the questions or comments of others. Nothing will end a productive discussion faster than feelings of inadequacy on the part of students. Many students are feeling out the facts of sexuality and AIDS as well as their own reactions to them. They are likely to have honest questions that are based on uninformed opinions and that may sound silly in light of sexual reality. Teachers and students alike should remember that all questions generally come from an honest curiosity and should be answered as fairly and concisely as possible.

4 Students Should Never Interrupt Others. This is actually a part of the "respect" ground rule above. Giving proper respect to others includes listening patiently and intently while they are talking. The class atmosphere must encourage students to feel free to express their ideas and opinions. Without a feeling of openness and a free flow of ideas and information, students can easily tune out of the lesson.

5 All Disagreement Must Be Polite. Respect and agreement can be two separate things, of course. Disagreement makes class discussion interesting and sometimes even enjoyable, but all disagreement must remain civil and polite. Debate and discussion should concern ideas, not personalities. If disagreement does occur, the class discussion should not be allowed to grow rude or nasty. Some students may initially worry that their contributions to the class might be ridiculed, so the teacher must do everything possible to help them feel comfortable and safe in their ideas. Quiet or shy students who otherwise might never speak up can offer valuable contributions to the class discussion. Also, teachers should remember that misperceptions some students may hold cannot be corrected if they are never heard.

6 Everyone Has the Right Not to Answer a Question. To keep students from feeling overwhelmed or threatened by what they might find to be an uncomfortable subject, teachers should allow students to avoid answering questions. Teachers must be careful about asking questions that could be perceived as personal or confidential, and should never intentionally put a student on the spot or ask too probing a question. Because we each have our own discomforts and embarrassments, teachers cannot always be sure which questions may be uncomfortable for students and which may not. Students should never be pressured into talking about an issue they would rather not talk about. Teachers should also feel free to exercise this rule if students ask uncomfortable questions of them. Many of the issues surrounding HIV and AIDS are quite personal, and teachers should establish their own limits of how much of their personal lives they are willing to discuss. If a student's question innocently crosses the line, teachers should not hesitate to call upon this ground rule.

7   We Will Not Seek Personal Information from Each Other. This ground rule will help head off the necessity of calling upon the sixth ground rule too often. If students know before the program begins that personal matters are off limits, they are less likely to attempt to ferret them out as the unit progresses. This ground rule, however, does not keep students or teachers from offering personal information if they choose to do so. It only limits the type of questions that are allowed to be asked of others.

Introducing the Unit

Even after more than ten years as a national concern, HIV and AIDS are still regarded by many people as a distant problem, something that happens to others. An important concept to establish as early as possible is that AIDS often strikes much closer to home than we expect. One college instructor overcame the potential distance her students might attempt to establish from the disease by writing on the board the names of all the people she had personally known who had died of AIDS-related diseases. To begin the class, she asked her students to add the names of their friends, relatives, or acquaintances who had also died of AIDS. In her class, the students were able to fill the board completely.[1] Although AIDS has hit some areas of the country quite hard, there are still a number of communities that have not had the same direct experience. Teachers in these areas may be aware of no friends or acquaintances who have been directly affected by AIDS. In such cases, it would be appropriate to cite the names of celebrities who have died of AIDS, such as Rock Hudson, Freddie Mercury, and Arthur Ashe. Students can then add any people they know of who have died as a result of AIDS, famous or otherwise. Teachers and students alike may be surprised at how quickly the list on the board grows. The point of this exercise is to prompt feelings of immediacy among students, to arouse in them sensations of a personal stake or loss because of AIDS. Celebrities have touched our lives, although perhaps not as deeply as friends or relatives. If students begin to relate to AIDS as a disease that strikes an individual and affects every person in that individual's life rather than as a collection of statistics, they will be more prepared to consider and make changes in their own lives.

MULTI MEDIA

One of the most obvious methods of presenting new material to students in interesting ways is through the use of various types of media. Videotape, film, overhead projectors, bulletin boards, and other vehicles for allowing students to see as well as hear about AIDS can prove quite effective in the beginning stages of the AIDS unit. A number of films and videotapes that spell out the facts and implications of AIDS are commercially available. Many of these also introduce students to methods of prevention and refusal skills. Films and videotapes are excellent ways of jumping into the topic without hesitation or embarrassment. Once the ball gets rolling, of course, teachers will find it easier to overcome such reluctance, because they will be carried along, at least to some extent, by the impetus of the film or videotape. As much as possible, teachers should try to use videotapes that reflect the students in their classroom. Adolescents pay more attention if their assigned role models are similar to themselves in age, ethnicity, and lifestyle. Inner-city students will not be impressed by a suburban high school quarterback who urges them to avoid drug use. They will relate to the characters of a videotape much more if they are able to see themselves when they look at the screen. AIDS prevention videotapes incorporate a variety of characters, so finding resources featuring the age, ethnic, and socioeconomic status reflected in a particular classroom is not difficult.

Teachers must be warned, however, not to let the videotape or film do too much of the work. Videotapes have only limited interactivity with students. While watching a videotape, students might formulate questions that the tape can never address. Likewise, the videotape might arouse fears or other emotions that can undermine students' understanding or openness. A videotape presenting facts about HIV and AIDS, no matter how well done, should never be allowed to stand on its own. At best, a videotape is an adjunct to the lesson. After viewing a videotape with the class, teachers should open the floor to discussion. What did students like or dislike? Did they agree with everything they saw, or were there a few points of disagreement? If so, what were those points, and why did students disagree? Such an approach to videotapes can produce rousing discussions and perhaps illuminate facts, emotions, or attitudes that were not presented as fully as they might have been. Effective teachers can even turn videotapes of only limited quality into successful teaching tools. If teachers are only able to procure videotapes that limit their presentation to abstinence and do not discuss safe-sex procedures, they can expand the discussion themselves by soliciting student critiques and comments about abstinence, safe sex, and the videotape's point of view.

Teachers who are more willing to initiate the AIDS unit themselves or who do not have the resources to obtain films or videotapes can find overhead projectors, bulletin boards, or felt boards quite useful as well. One popular theme of such visual aids is to present the body as a well-defended fortress with HIV and other viruses or infections as invading armies. White blood cells, or T cells, can be represented as generals directing soldiers to fight off the infections. Most infections, again using colds or the flu as examples, can be defeated. HIV, on the other hand, can be portrayed graphically as getting past the soldiers and undermining the T-cell generals, much as spies try to do in actual warfare. A bulletin board can offer a static representation of this scene, while felt boards or overhead projectors allow a limited amount of movement and change. Actual representations of the body and its viral invaders can also be displayed through posters or bulletin boards, either in conjunction with the previous example or by themselves. The actual health effects of HIV to the body may be better understood by students if the fortress-and-invader metaphor introduces the concept in the first place.

Teachers can also use such visual aids to introduce the proper names for the various parts of the body they will discuss. These names can best be assigned to their respective parts of the body visually than by attempting to describe the various functions these parts fulfill. This exercise, best presented in a temporary medium such as an overhead projector or felt board rather than a more permanent bulletin board that students, teachers, and visitors might find uncomfortable after a day or two, is most effective with younger students. Many young students have not yet become used to hearing slang terms for body parts and can learn the proper names for the first time. Older students, accustomed to slang or impolite language for parts of the body, may find it more difficult to shift their language. Teachers of these older students should strive as much as possible to make proper names the appropriate terms to use in class, but should not be so insistent as to allow students' use of slang terms to undermine the communication of necessary information and concepts.

GROUP ACTIVITIES

Many teachers have discovered that they have more success in engaging their students in new material if they employ activities that allow students to work together. Insights provided by other students can bring a new level of understanding to the material.

Cooperative Learning

One instructional method for groups that has resulted in success in teaching about HIV and AIDS is cooperative learning, in which students help each other uncover relevant facts and information.[2] Theories about cooperative learning have been common in educational circles since before AIDS began to be recognized and have been used with students of all ages and in all subjects. This technique certainly is not limited to AIDS education, but it does offer particular qualities that can help with this subject. Because AIDS education is concerned with more than simply conveying information and extends to influencing social skills and attitudes toward others, cooperative learning can be especially suited to this material.

The effectiveness of cooperative learning comes from the fact that all participants take turns performing the roles of both teacher and student. The participation of all students in a group is necessary for any of the students to learn all the material. This technique should not be confused with peer education or peer tutoring. No one student will have all the information necessary to complete the task at hand, so no student is in the position of being the only teacher to the others. Instead, everyone learns from everyone else.

Cooperative learning groups are commonly made up of four to six students. These groups are given an assignment to complete, and each group member has some, but not all, of the information necessary to do that. When a class is split into cooperative learning groups, the teacher can give every group the same exercise or give different groups different assignments. If groups are given different assignments, a representative of each group should make a report to the class at large so that other students are able to benefit from the knowledge each group has uncovered.

When teachers are preparing to utilize cooperative learning techniques, they should make sure that student groups are as heterogenous as possible. Part of the point of cooperative learning is to expose students to as wide a variety of people, backgrounds, skills, attitudes, and levels of achievement as possible. Students complete their assignment by cooperating and building consensus, both of which become more challenging if students represent a cross-section of the classroom, rather than a mere corner of it. Cliques and in-groups, complete with leaders and hierarchies, have always been a part of schools. Cooperative learning groups attempt to do away with both of these elements in favor of allowing students to share leadership in a more egalitarian atmosphere. If teachers simply allow students to be grouped with their friends, the existing hierarchy will be preserved and students will not have the opportunity to stretch as they might have in a differently constituted group. By promoting interaction among students who normally do not mingle, teachers are potentially exposing them to new attitudes and ideas, and helping them to sharpen their social skills. Exposure to new thoughts and outlooks assists students in broadening their respect and acceptance of others, which, along with influencing behavior and expanding knowledge, is a goal of AIDS education.

After dividing the class into heterogenous groups, teachers should make the assignments. A simple method for teachers to monitor the assignments might be to pass out packets containing the assignments and information sources. The assignments for each group can be as simple as a list of questions needing to be answered or as complicated as researching and writing a detailed report to be presented to the class. The questions asked of groups can be about any factual material concerning AIDS and HIV—transmission, protection, risk, symptoms, myths, or any other facet the teacher wishes to explore. The sources for the information, however, may require a bit of preparation on the teacher's part. A few accessible sources of information for older students are currently available, such as *AIDS: Trading Fears for Facts* by Karen Hein and Theresa Foy DiGeronimo and *What You Can Do to Avoid AIDS* by Earvin "Magic" Johnson.[3] These books are appropriate for teenagers, and will allow them to find the information and answers they need for their assignment. Journal articles concerning HIV and AIDS might offer some interest for more advanced students, but they are often densely written and inaccessible for nontechnical readers. Teachers would need to perform quite a bit of legwork to locate and gather them. Still, for teachers willing to make the effort, these journal articles will help students move one step closer to current AIDS research.

Younger children may be a bit put off by the amount and explicitness of the information that many books about AIDS provide, and might be better served by an information sheet compiled by the teacher. In preparing the information sheet, teachers should summarize the necessary facts that students are to uncover. Teachers can provide different information sheets to different group members, so that no one member has all the information necessary to complete the exercise. If different groups have different assignments, information sheets can have some facts appropriate for more than one group, therefore allowing students to sift through all the information in order to find that which applies to their own activity.

When only one or two members of a four-person group has the answer or the means to uncover the answer to a question that each must fill in, the group members begin to cooperate and negotiate with each other to procure all the information they need. This allows students to interact with the material at a deeper level than they otherwise would in listening to a lecture or even watching a videotape. When groups have questions concerning the assignment, teachers must be careful not to provide too much information in response. At most, teachers should facilitate students in finding the information without actually showing students where the information can be found.

Because this technique is a departure from what students are used to, some students may have a bit of trouble adjusting to it. Teachers should try to remain aware of what is taking place within each group. If necessary, teachers can intervene in a group to encourage cooperation, smooth out any rough relationships, and even out the level of participation if one group member is exerting too much control or chooses not to join in the activity. Because cooperation is the purpose of the exercise, teachers should address these problems diplomatically, convincing and encouraging students to follow through on the assignment rather than simply commanding them to follow instructions.

After cooperative learning groups complete their information gathering, teachers have a number of options as to where to take the task next. The groups could make presentations of their material to the rest of the class, allowing all students to be exposed to the information, and allowing the presenting students to have another opportunity to interact with their particular facts. Some educators have suggested that information gathering be followed up by role-playing activities to help personalize the facts a bit more.[4] If a group were answering questions about risky behaviors, for example, they might be given a role-play in which a character named Joe tries to talk his girlfriend, Elaine, into having unprotected sex with him. The actual scenario provided by the teacher need be no longer than that. The other group members could role-play friends who try to help talk the couple through their dilemma. After a few practice runs, maybe with group members trading roles back and forth, the group can perform their role-play for the rest of the class. Utilizing this method allows students in each group as well as their classmates to apply the information they have gathered and learned, helping them realize that it applies to real life and not just to the classroom. Role-playing as a teaching device to encourage the growth of decision-making skills, refusal skills, and other social skills will be explored in greater detail in a later chapter.

Transmission

Many teachers will want to convey information to their students by engaging in types of group activities other than cooperative learning, and a number of possibilities exist. One exercise that dramatically demonstrates the threat of exposure to HIV is called "Coupon Swap Meet." In preparing this activity, teachers must obtain a small slip of paper, or "coupon," perhaps three inches square, for each student in the class. Teachers should number off coupons *1*, *2*, *3*, up through *10*, so that each numeral appears on the same quantity of coupons. If, for instance, a class has thirty students, the numeral *1* will appear on three coupons, the numeral *2* on three, and so forth. If the number of students in the class is not divisible by ten, then some numerals will appear on one fewer coupon than others. Fold each coupon down the middle so that the numeral cannot be seen.

During class, students should place a clean piece of paper and a pen or pencil on their desk or table. The coupons should be distributed, one to a student. They can be passed out by the teacher or a student, or they can be tossed into a shoe box so that students can each choose their own. When students have received one coupon apiece, they should unfold it, look at the numeral, and copy that numeral onto their clean sheet of paper. After every student has noted the number of their coupon, they should be invited to swap coupons with one other person, writing the number of the new coupon under the first on the sheet of paper. Some students may swap coupons only to receive the same number again. This does not matter. Next, a third swap should be arranged following the same pattern: students write their new number below the first two. At the end of these swaps, every student should have written down three numbers; some students may have three different numbers, while others might repeat a number.

The teacher should next ask which students had a particular number, in our example the number 5. Because the distribution of the numbers on coupons is fairly equal, three students passing a number 5 coupon twice should result in nine students having received it. When the nine students have identified themselves, the teacher should announce that the numeral 5 represented HIV. All students who had written down that numeral had been exposed to the virus. From three infected students in a class of thirty, the virus quickly expanded to a total of nine students. This activity provides a very dramatic demonstration of how HIV can spread swiftly and silently. It also demonstrates the innocence and ignorance often involved in HIV infection. No student traded coupons with someone they thought might be carrying the infected number. If teachers oversee more than one section of AIDS education at a time, they may want to vary the assigned number so that students in one section cannot warn students in a later section about which number to avoid.

An interesting variation on this activity is for the teacher to announce a second swap in which the number representing HIV is identified before the swap begins. Students will suddenly become very careful about who they are willing to trade coupons with and will gain some insight into the social ostracism and rejection that people with AIDS often experience.

Truth versus Myth

Since before it was even properly identified, AIDS has been the subject of rumors and false statements. Many of these rumors have remained in the public consciousness and have risen to the power of myth. These are falsehoods that have often been taken as fact. An effective method of ferreting out these myths and separating them from truth is to present them to the class for examination. Every student should be invited to write down a statement they have heard about HIV or AIDS to be gathered by the teacher and then randomly passed out again for other students to read. Students may write down a statement they know to be true or false, or one about which they are unsure. The point of the activity is to underscore the facts and debunk the myths.

One student might write down that AIDS is transmitted through infected blood. This of course is true. The class, students and teacher together, can discuss this fact and its various implications. Just because a statement is true does not mean that the teacher should pass by it quickly to move on to something else. Another student may write that HIV can be transmitted by mosquito bites. This, as we know, is a myth, but it is a myth taken as truth by a large number of people. Teachers should not allow students to ridicule or make fun of whoever might write such a statement. Because students have been asked to write down "a statement they have heard," the student offering the mosquito statement may have offered it knowing that it is false. Each class, however, likely houses more than a few students who do not have all the facts of AIDS straight, and potential derision will not encourage them to seek correct answers. The anonymity of writing statements that will later be read aloud by others offers an extra protective layer to those students who may be embarrassed to ask the questions that are on their minds.

As much as possible, teachers should allow their students to guide the discussion, only breaking in to provide direction and correction if myths are not being exposed. Whenever possible, allowing students to discover the truth on their own will provide a more persuasive lesson. If they are able to discuss the offered statements of truth and myth thoroughly, students will be able to work through any misunderstandings or misconceptions they may have.

Assessing Personal Risk

Using the same system of gathering anonymous statements from students to be read anonymously is an effective way to initiate discussion on actual student risk for HIV infection. Teachers can ask students to answer one or both of the following questions:

Why am I at risk for HIV infection?

Why am I not at risk for HIV infection?

These questions are not necessarily mutually exclusive. The same student may have compelling answers for each of these questions.

If teachers are willing to accept that some of their students are sexually active, they might augment these questions with two more:

Why do I practice safer sex?

Why do I not practice safer sex?

Because this is likely to be a subject highly charged with emotion, teachers will have to be very careful in how they carry it out. Essentially, this exercise asks students to confront their own attitudes and behavior in regard to what can be a very dangerous subject. Self-examination can be very useful in AIDS education, but if the examination forces students to confront behaviors that are too frightening, the end result might simply be more denial of risk. If a teacher feels that the class as a whole will not be supportive and open to realistically discussing risk behaviors in which some of the class members may be participating, this activity might best be omitted. However, for the classes that are willing to attempt this activity, the self-searching and potential recognition of risk that accompany it will provide a powerful and sobering experience.

Although it seems certain that higher-grade classes will contain sexually active students, teachers should also be careful about possible parental reaction against open discussion of students' sexuality. Sexual behavior is one of those subjects that might be acceptable as long as the discussion remains generalized, but it becomes less acceptable if the dialogue moves toward the specific. Even though anonymity is an important element in this activity, just the simple fact that the discussion relates to the behavior of someone in the room may be too much for some parents to accept.

Graphic Arts

Some of the old standbys of education over the years have been graphic arts displays such as posters and bulletin boards. Posters and other graphic arts allow students to use their creativity to internalize and better understand the material they are attempting to portray. When students work in groups on such projects, they also benefit from the shared experience with and insights from each other. Posters and bulletin boards are different media, of course, and they serve different functions. Posters generally require less effort and can be made quickly using Magic Markers, crayons, and cut-out pictures. Teachers can choose to provide either poster board or simple construction paper as a base for the poster, depending on the ambition of the project.

Teachers can divide the students up into several groups and assign different aspects of HIV and AIDS for each group to depict. Groups can concentrate on transmission, risky behaviors, risk reduction and prevention, or other elements of AIDS education that teachers might think appropriate for their particular classes. Working together in the groups, students can research the pertinent facts of their assigned element of AIDS, develop a basic theme, design artwork, come up with any slogans or other texts, and put it all together on the poster.

Teachers should decide on the appropriate amount of time to devote to making posters and should provide materials suitable to that decision. If, for example, teachers want to set aside more than an hour, they would want to make sure students are using a sturdy poster board that will last longer than construction paper. Further, teachers should encourage a high level of ambition among students to create posters they feel would be worthy of adorning the classroom walls for the span of the AIDS education unit. For teachers working with younger children or teachers who want to make the posters a quick exercise of an hour or less, construction paper can be an easy substitute for poster board. At the end of the class period, students who have made posters that will not be displayed in the classroom should be allowed to take their work home.

Bulletin boards, of course, are a more elaborate form of poster. Some teachers, particularly those of late elementary school children, have a policy of allowing students to create themselves or help their teacher create themed bulletin boards around the classroom. This would be an excellent opportunity for some students to use their creativity on the bulletin boards to learn about HIV and AIDS themselves, and to pass that knowledge on to other students through their artwork.

Hotline Operator

During the initial fact-finding phase of AIDS education, teachers must be sure not to forget their goal of fostering understanding and acceptance of those infected with HIV. "Hotline Operator" allows students to review and apply the facts of HIV and AIDS and provides them with an opportunity to look into the experience of those who fear they may be infected with HIV and seek information and advice from an AIDS hotline. Students divide into groups, where they are confronted by questions that would potentially be asked by callers to an AIDS hotline. Because the class is only simulating the atmosphere of an actual hotline, they need not respond with immediate answers but can be given time to confer and even conduct research if necessary. This activity can also take the form of written questions to allow written responses. Teachers can determine how much time can be allotted to this activity. Teachers with access to a speakerphone can participate in the National AIDS Hotline's Classroom Calls program, which allows the entire class to be able to talk to the Hotline. Teachers should call 1-800-342-AIDS to make arrangements for this activity.

Teachers who are interested in challenging their students further might use this context for a form of role-play. In groups of only two or three, one student can take on the part of hotline caller with the other students standing in for the operator. With a caller "on the line," operators must think on their feet, keeping the caller from hanging up but providing correct and useful information. Students can devise their own questions, or teachers can provide scenarios for the caller to use, such as a teenager who fears a classmate might be HIV positive, someone asking whether HIV can be transmitted through kissing, a person whose best friend has just tested HIV positive, or someone worried about being infected and contemplating taking a test for the HIV antibody. Some of these scenarios may draw quite emotional responses from students, so teachers should observe the interaction closely. Understanding, sensitivity, and compassion toward those whose lives have been touched by HIV and AIDS are important goals of AIDS education, but upsetting individual students should not be part of the plan. Many students will have to confront the disease in their lives, and such confrontation in the security of the classroom provides a sort of safety net for emotions. Still, teachers should be careful that classroom activity does not provoke any students to respond too emotionally.

Game Show

Just as the title of this activity suggests, students divide into teams and compete by answering questions about HIV and AIDS. The number of students in a class will help determine the number of teams. Teams should ideally be made up of four to six students. Larger teams than this will allow some students to sit in the background without having to answer any questions; smaller teams will put too much pressure on individual students, who, unable to fall back on other team members, will have to answer most or all questions themselves. Teachers can play the M.C., asking the questions and keeping the game going, or they can pass that responsibility on to a student. Questions should remain strictly informational, with clear right and wrong answers. Easier questions can be worth a small number of points while more challenging questions would be worth more. Teachers can establish a time limit for each game or a goal toward which each team will amass points.

To capture the spirit and fun of game shows, each team or team member should be given some sort of signaling device. A buzzer or a bell will work nicely, but if teachers are concerned about too much noise, a flashlight can easily fill the bill as well. To promote teamwork, teachers can give only one signal device to a team so that teams provide consensus answers. If every team member has an individual signal device, each student should be responsible for providing his or her own answer after signaling.

A tournament can be set up for teams, and if several sections of AIDS education are being taught at the same time, the tournament can even involve several classes. Such a tournament can provide an excellent opportunity for students to review and reinforce the information necessary for an understanding of the disease and its effects. There are certainly enough facets of AIDS information to support a number of different questions for such a tournament, so teachers will not have to simply repeat the same information over and over.

Debates

Older students can hold debates about various medical, social, and political issues that relate to HIV and AIDS. A debate is an excellent forum in which many sides of difficult questions can be examined. Following the lead of high school debate tournaments, teachers can assign two debaters to a team that will argue either the positive or negative side of a posed question. Teachers might have several teams debate the same question or offer different questions to different teams. AIDS and HIV offer many ethical dilemmas that can generate lively discussions, such as the issues of mandatory testing, doctor-patient confidentiality, and disclosure to employers, to identify only a few.

Just as is the practice in tournament debating, teachers can carefully time the speeches, allowing each team a few minutes to make their own argument and respond to the argument of the other team. The amount of time given to each speaker will determine how long the debate itself will last. Traditional team debate offers each of two teammates two opportunities to speak. The first speaker debating the positive side of the question sets up his team's arguments in about four or five minutes. The first negative speaker responds to these arguments for the same amount of time, and the second positive speaker answers this response and attempts to clarify the positive arguments further. Finally, the second negative speaker gets a chance to tear down the positive argument. Each speaker usually gets a second, shorter amount of time in which to speak again, often two or three minutes. Teachers are invited to modify this framework in any manner that makes it more useful to their classrooms. Tournament debate, of course, features an established scoring system to determine the winner of the debate, but class debates might best be decided by a vote of students.

Teachers have a great deal of discretion as to how much time to allot for this activity. They can modify the amount of time debaters are allowed to speak or the quantity of preparation time they provide. If teachers want to see a reasonably well-thought-out, detailed debate, they can give teams their assigned questions at the beginning of one class period and devote the rest of that class to research. Students can then complete any unfinished research after class and begin the debate in the following class period. Teachers more interested in challenging their students to think on their feet can grant less time for preparation and begin the debate sooner. Students, those debating and those listening, will benefit from the exchange of ideas and information and will be prodded to think the issues through for themselves.

AIDS-Prevention Videotape

Technology has allowed teachers to have a great amount of freedom and variety in the kinds of activities they can provide for their students. The new tool with perhaps the largest potential for creativity is the video camera. Bringing a video camera into the AIDS classroom opens up the opportunity for students to do any number of creative things: making a video promoting protective behavior, presenting the facts in a visually inventive manner, writing and acting in a scene about HIV and AIDS, writing a song or rap and shooting a music video.

In many ways, shooting a video is a fancier, more technical version of making a poster. An effective video, of course, requires more complex thinking to make the larger project clear and understandable, but students are essentially flexing the same group of mental muscles. Different schools will have different resources, and some teachers will be able to divide their classes into two or more groups, while others will have to keep the class together for this project.

Making a video demands a much larger amount of preparation than many of the activities we have already surveyed. Classes can be divided into groups to get ready for the video. One group should come up with the scenario and script. If students are intending to shoot an informational, fact-based video, they may wonder why a script is necessary. Remind them that even news documentaries have scripts to determine the order and the manner in which the facts will be presented. Another group, the main spokespersons or actors, must prepare their performance. Someone must decide where the video will be shot and what, if any, costumes, props, or backgrounds will be necessary. As soon as a teacher can procure a video camera, the students responsible for shooting the video should practice and learn how to use it effectively. As they will discover, it is much easier simply to hold a camera and point it in the right direction than to preplan a shot or sequence and make sure that everyone and everything is in the correct position doing the correct activity. As in professional filmmaking, the more these decisions are made up front and the more prepared the students are, the faster and more problem-free the video shoot will become.

During the video shoot, every student should have some sort of job. The students in front of the camera and holding and shooting the camera have obvious jobs, of course, but a number of other jobs are necessary. A script supervisor can be used to keep track of what must be shot next and to prepare for that shot. A prop keeper makes sure that every prop is where it needs to be when it needs to be. A costume supervisor will take care of any costume changes that are necessary and make sure that the proper costumes are used. One student might be assigned to oversee all of these technical aspects of the video. One student or a group of students must also be assigned to direct the film, showing the actors what to do and how to deliver their lines, and showing the cameraperson where to stand and how to move the camera if necessary. This all sounds much more complicated than it actually is, and teachers are encouraged to help their students experiment with the message they want to send and the method by which they want to send it. Students are likely to find the experience quite enjoyable, and teachers might even have fun with it as well.

Questions

One of the basics of education is answering questions. Socrates asked questions of his students to encourage them to think and reason out their own answers. Students also have questions, and skilled teachers can help them answer these questions through the students' own logical thinking and research if necessary. Inductive and deductive reasoning are both learned processes, and teachers must be available and willing to help their students.

Answering questions is also an important element of AIDS education. We have previously reviewed activities that can help students recognize the difference between the truth and the myths of AIDS, but that activity might not be enough to assuage all the fears or correct all the misinformation that students may have. Teachers should build time into every class period to answer questions students may have. Because of the delicate nature of the subject, however, teachers should not assume that their students will compete with each other to ask any questions. If students are still not clear on a particular concept, they will not want to announce it to all their classmates. If students are embarrassed about the personal nature of the worries they have over AIDS, they are likewise unlikely to proclaim it before all their friends. For these reasons, teachers should institute some form of anonymous questioning so that students can seek the information they desire without fear of embarrassment or ridicule.

We have already seen the effectiveness of anonymity in the Truth versus Myth and Assessing Personal Risk activities, and similar benefits can be gained with anonymity here as well. As some questions may concern AIDS myths or personal risk, these activities may answer a few questions before students have an opportunity to ask them. As soon as possible after completing those exercises, however, student questions should be invited and encouraged. Teachers might replicate the process of asking students to write down a question about HIV or AIDS that they brought with them into the classroom or one that is drawn from that day's classroom activity, and redistributing them for other students to read, thus maintaining anonymity. Putting the questions out before the class also allows other students to provide answers when they are able. Such an activity, however, can turn out to be quite time consuming, depending on the complexity of the questions. Teachers might prefer to gather and read the questions themselves in order to skip over redundant, inappropriate, or overly personal questions. Whenever possible, teachers should respond to personal questions on a one-on-one basis in order to avoid any shame or humiliation on the part of the student seeking an answer. When such questions are asked anonymously, however, teachers may not always be able to identify where they came from. Unless absolutely sure of the source, teachers should not take it upon themselves to presume to identify a particular student. Singling out the wrong student to whom to provide a personal answer, even in private, can leave the true questioner without the answer to an important inquiry and the misidentified student confused and embarrassed to have been taken aside in order to hear about someone else's personal situation.

Anonymous questions will remain important as the unit progresses, but it would obviously take up too much time at the end of each class period to repeat this procedure every day. Instead, teachers might adapt a practice familiar from business. Instead of a "suggestion box," teachers can place a "question box" at a prominent place in the classroom so that students can anonymously write down their questions and slip them into the box sometime before, during, or after class. At the end of the day, teachers can review the questions and determine which they should answer during the next class period. Teachers can decide whether each class should open or close with questions. Beginning class with the previous day's questions can help clarify issues previously covered and lay the groundwork for that day's material. Some teachers, however, may fear that dwelling on questions from previous classes at the beginning of a new class period may detract from the material at hand and may choose to hold questions until the ending of class. This practice makes it possible for some questions to be answered by the new material presented during class. Either time is fine as long as the questions are addressed. Clear understanding of the risks associated with AIDS and the potential protective behaviors is vital before students will actually practice that behavior. Most of the questions, even if they seem silly on the surface, are important to the students who have asked them. They represent real concerns, and answering them helps the teacher establish credibility as someone who is interested in making sure students have all the facts.The more openly teachers answer questions from the question box, the more students will trust the opinions and information teachers share about HIV and AIDS.

SOLITARY ACTIVITIES

For the most part, if a class's group activities are effective, teachers will find very little need to provide in-class activities for students to complete individually. Interaction among students in the group activities described above should allow every student to become involved in actively learning about HIV and AIDS. Some teachers, however, might want to have a few individual activities on hand for groups that finish early or for students to complete outside of class. The following are a few suggestions.

Puzzles

Teachers can put word-search or crossword puzzles together fairly quickly for their students, using important words from HIV and AIDS education. Words like "virus," "immune," "deficient," "blood," "acquire," and "needle," or for older students, "condom," "bleach," "semen," "penis," "vagina," and other words that teachers feel are appropriate can be included with simple definitions in a crossword puzzle for students to do in their spare time. Using graph paper as a grid, teachers can write the words horizontally or vertically, allowing them to intersect whenever possible. Number the first square of each new word left to right, top to bottom. Next, write a corresponding definition for each word. Crossword puzzles can reinforce AIDS vocabulary and definitions. In fact, this activity can also help reinforce the correct anatomical names for parts of the body.

Word-search puzzles are even easier for teachers to design than crosswords. A border can be drawn to create a square or rectangle on the same type of graph paper used for the crossword puzzle. Once the boundaries have been established, teachers can fill the grid with words horizontally, vertically, diagonally, and backwards. When teachers have included all the words they intend to, the empty spaces on the grid can be filled with random letters so that no spaces are left blank. Teachers should be sure to keep a separate list of the words they have included so students will be able to find them all. While crossword puzzles can be created by hand, word-search puzzles are sometimes better created on a typewriter or computer so that the spaces are all uniform and the letters are easy for students to read.

Teachers might also invite students to create their own crossword or word-search puzzles. This will allow them to interact with the AIDS vocabulary on an even deeper level than simply filling in the blanks of someone else's puzzle.

Reviewing Risk

As an alternative to the group activity assessing and talking about risky behaviors discussed previously, teachers might prefer to use a personal and more private worksheet. The worksheet can list a number of behaviors and ask students to rate them on the basis of risk for infection by HIV. The rating scale can use numbers ("1" for no risk, "2" for possible risk, "3" for definite risk) or letters ("A," no risk, "B," possible risk, "C," definite risk). The definite risk category should include obvious activities such as sharing IV needles, having unprotected sex, and others we have already discussed. Possible risk activities might include deep or French kissing, cleaning needles before sharing them, drinking or using drugs to a point of intoxication, having protected sex, and other activities that carry varying levels of risk. Safe activities can consist of swimming in a swimming pool, eating a meal at the same table as someone who is HIV positive, being bitten by a mosquito, hugging or shaking hands with an HIV-positive person, playing sports with someone of uncertain infection status, and so one. Teachers will likely want to discuss this material, and because it involves activities and circumstances offered by the teacher rather than by the personal experience of students, the students themselves are less likely to feel personally threatened by the discussion. It can be very traumatic for students to realize they are behaving in such a way as to put them at risk for HIV infection, so teachers, without inappropriately prying, should observe student behaviors very closely during this activity. It would also be appropriate for teachers to let students know that they or other professional counselors are available for discussion or counseling about any issues that concern students as a result of this activity.

AIDS Hotline

Another group activity that can be converted to an exercise for solitary students is "Hotline Operator." In the group activity, of course, students act as hotline operators to answer questions posed by other students. As a take-home assignment, students can assume the other side and actually call the National AIDS Hotline to ask their own questions of the real operators there. These questions can concern information that has not yet been covered in class or facts that students have perhaps not understood during class. To make sure students complete this assignment, they can turn in their questions and the answers supplied by the AIDS hotline operator. Two or three questions per student should be plenty.

This exercise will help students take the entire process of AIDS information more seriously. Its intent is primarily to give the students the experience of calling the AIDS hotline rather than the discovery of the actual information they are able to glean from the operators. Many people call the National AIDS Hotline when they have some concern over the possibility of their own infection with HIV or that of friends or relatives. Calling the hotline as a class assignment can help build empathy and understanding with those who do have some cause for worry about HIV and AIDS. Also, by gaining familiarity with the hotline now, students will be in a better position to call the AIDS hotline for information on behalf of themselves or a friend or relative if the necessity arises some time in the future. Teachers should point out one of the most attractive features of the National AIDS Hotline, which is its anonymity. Some students who have honest concerns about HIV as a result of AIDS education may be uncomfortable coming forward to discuss their worries with their classroom teacher. Teachers can encourage such students by making sure that all students in the class realize that the anonymity of the AIDS hotline is always an option for them. It is far more important to address students' concerns than to make sure these concerns follow school channels.

Teachers should also be prepared to pick up and discuss small bits of interesting information that students discover in talking to the AIDS operators. Gaining new facts and details is not the primary intention of this activity, as stated above, but if students find material that engages them, it could nudge the class discussion toward relevant subject areas that the teacher might have overlooked.

Writing

Writing assignments can be appropriate in virtually any subject area and can especially be used by teachers introducing short bursts of AIDS instruction into their classes. English teachers can close a discussion of AIDS with an assignment to write about social, political, or other aspects of AIDS. For teachers who want to address the subject but do not wish it to occupy their instructional time, writing assignments intended to improve students' composition skills can offer various features of AIDS, along with other potential areas of student interest, as essay subjects. Social studies classes might look into the psychology of the AIDS crisis and have students explore and express their own feelings about the disease and its impact. Political science classes are an obvious outlet for essays on social policy concerning HIV and AIDS. Biology classes can study the medical manifestations of AIDS, and history classes might investigate medical epidemics of the past.

Teachers delivering a full, multiclass unit on HIV and AIDS might consider asking their students to keep AIDS journals of their thoughts and responses to material presented in class. These journals might contain fears, hopes, and ruminations students experience during the unit. Writing assignments such as this demand that students actively participate and interact with the material. Under optimum conditions, students will also deeply consider the information and material they confront during the unit and develop their own ideas concerning it. Some students might consider how they would react if they or someone close to them was found to be HIV positive. Others could contemplate volunteering their time to serve with various community service organizations focused on AIDS. Journal writing can help students sort through and understand the emotions they encounter when confronting this highly charged subject matter. Teachers can assign the writing to be performed outside class or, in order to encourage the journals further, they can devote five or ten minutes during class to these. If students can get started during class, thoughts and ideas might be triggered to make them even more enthusiastic about completing the assignment later.

At the end of the unit, AIDS journals can be taken up and graded by teachers. Teachers should be careful in assigning grades to what may be personal material, however. Some students may have developed ideas different from what their teachers expected, and they certainly should not be penalized for that. What teachers should mostly examine in the journals is the effort students have put forth. Students who have merely jotted down perfunctory comments with little obvious consideration should be given lower grades than those who have honestly confronted the subject matter. Any honorable efforts students have made should be commended through higher grades and more positive teacher comments. In reviewing these AIDS journals, teachers should also watch for points of view that they have not yet considered or perhaps have not even encountered. Students often have a unique viewpoint because of their age and experience, and teachers should certainly be prepared to find new sparks of interest or inventive approaches to the subject matter that they might utilize when teaching future classes on HIV and AIDS. Teachers, of course, will initially be working out the kinks of their AIDS unit as they go along, and they should try to keep their minds as open and sensitive to student response as possible. Students are often very candid in their reactions to the efficacy of various teaching strategies, and teachers would do well to pay attention. Teachers themselves have a unique opportunity to learn a lot about how AIDS should be taught by listening to their students.

LECTURE AND INFORMATION DELIVERY

Although we have often stated that lectures should be replaced by other information-gathering activities as often as possible, some amount of lecturing will probably be utilized by most teachers. Lectures should be as engaging and interesting as possible. Visual aids, as discussed earlier, are always helpful in keeping students' attention. Another method that some teachers might find useful is to invite guest "experts" to speak to their classes. Two potential pools of experts will be discussed here.

Doctors and Medical Personnel

Very few groups of people are more up-to-date on the latest AIDS information than members of the medical community. Physicians, nurses, and other health care workers have access to new research and medical studies and can help teachers and their students understand the basic physical facts of HIV. Teachers are certainly advised to seek out health care workers to help them understand all the implications of HIV and AIDS. However, many physicians and nurses have begun to make their own presence felt in the classroom. Vital information about HIV and AIDS can be presented very effectively by community-minded medical personnel. Doctors and nurses carry an authority on medical issues that teachers simply cannot replicate. During the purely informational phase of AIDS education, medical workers can provide facts and details and can specifically answer what might be obscure questions for a teacher. In many communities, some health care workers may have already announced their willingness and availability to talk to classes or even to individual students about HIV, AIDS, risky behaviors, and potential methods of protecting themselves. Medical personnel who themselves have young children or teenagers may be particularly eager to offer their services. Such speakers, however, may not be experienced in addressing groups of children or adolescents. They may need a bit of coaching from teachers to help them keep their presentation interesting and at a level easily understood by the lay audience. As teachers know, the easiest way to lose an adolescent audience is to become long-winded and dull. Another pitfall medical speakers should be advised to avoid is the problem of appearing too authoritarian. Students do not want to be pronounced upon and preached to, they want to be informed. Outside speakers can be most effective if they let their information, which is sobering enough by itself, stand on its own. Students will remain attentive as long as the speaker appears to deserve their attention.

When seeking out potential medical speakers, however, teachers should stick fairly closely to AIDS clinics or hospitals known for their AIDS care. Unfortunately, even after all the time AIDS has been a public issue, some medical workers remain unwilling to treat patients for AIDS-related symptoms and diseases and refuse to inform themselves about the disease. Teachers are advised to contact health care professionals who are likely to share their concern over educating students to protect themselves from infection.

Another possible source for medical speakers might be local medical schools. Students training to enter the health professions are often very willing to participate in projects that help the community. Speaking to junior high school and high school classes can also help the med students practice their skills in meeting with the public and explaining difficult medical situations in simple language. Some medical schools already participate in such public outreach. A program called Students Teaching AIDS to Students (STATS) was started by the American Medical Students Association in 1988 to train and encourage students in medical school to help adolescents understand the perils of HIV infection. Besides simply discussing the facts of HIV and AIDS, these med students also discuss teenage attitudes and behaviors that can lead to unintended infection. Most med students are in their early twenties, not much older than the teens themselves. Students in med school are certainly closer to their teen years than practicing health professionals. Because of their age, many of these med students will remember the pressures and problems of adolescence, allowing them to closely identify with the teenagers they are trying to reach. Therefore, med students are likely to be able to strike a balance between medical authority and adolescent identification. If a local medical school is affiliated with STATS or has a similar program on its own, it could provide an excellent resource for teachers to use in disseminating the facts about HIV and AIDS.

HIV-Positive Speakers

Unfortunately, one effective group of speakers on the subject of HIV and AIDS is growing daily. That group is, of course, individuals who are infected with the virus. Speakers infected with HIV can be most effective in putting a face on the virus and bringing the consequences closer to home for students. If adolescents are able to have a personal experience with an HIV-positive person, they will immediately be confronted with the human side of the statistics. It is far too easy for students, and anyone else for that matter, to distance themselves from the abstract facts and figures that surround this virus and disease. Anything that helps make these concepts more concrete is a boon to AIDS education. HIV-positive speakers can quite easily offer practical facts and information about HIV and AIDS, but their primary usefulness to teachers will be in affecting student attitudes about the disease. Students need to understand that this infection can indeed happen to them, and what better method of bringing that fact home than to introduce them to someone to whom it has happened. Another benefit of inviting HIV-positive speakers into the classroom is that it will lower students' anxiety about associating socially with people with AIDS. Just as students with HIV-positive friends or relatives have a lower level of worry over becoming casually infected with the virus themselves, students who are allowed to interact with HIV-positive people in the classroom will learn that they have nothing to fear from casual contact with them. Their acceptance of HIV-positive individuals will rise, allowing them to set aside their prejudices and anxieties.

The speaking skills of HIV-positive presenters are quite important to their effectiveness. Good speakers can hold the class in their hands, emoting and inspiring students. Teachers are well aware that

poor speakers, no matter what their particular expertise or knowledge may be, can distance, bore, and alienate students, and thus undermine any effect they might be seeking. This same principle is
true of HIV-positive speakers. If they are boring, they will convey no
message at all to students, who will be left with the same expectations of invulnerability and the same prejudices against HIV-positive
people. A good speaker, on the other hand, will personalize the risk
of HIV infection, make students think twice about their own chances
for infection, and increase their compassion and acceptance for people already infected with the virus. There has been some discussion
among some educators about finding an HIV-infected speaker as demographically close to the majority of students as possible, that is,
adolescent and heterosexual. The more characteristics a speaker
shares with his or her audience, the argument goes, the easier it will
be for the audience to identify with the speaker. This theory certainly makes sense, and teachers should attempt to find speakers
who resemble their students. The goal of similarity should not over-
ride the aim of finding a captivating speaker, however. A poor lec-
turer who differs demographically from students is likely the poorest
choice a teacher can make. However, a good speaker who is older
and otherwise different from students may be a better choice than a
heterosexual adolescent who has trouble communicating the realities of HIV infection. Teenagers are well practiced in noticing differences between themselves and others, and they will not hesitate to
embrace someone with whom they would like to identify or distance
themselves from someone with whom they would not. An effective
speaker will inspire more identification than one who is ineffective,
no matter what other features they may possess.

HIV-positive speakers can be found in local AIDS community
service groups. Teachers determined to find HIV-positive adolescents
who are ethnically similar to the students in their classes may have a
harder time than teachers who are more open to the speakers various service organizations can provide. For exactly the reasons we
have discussed earlier, HIV-positive adolescents are not always easy
to find. Although teenagers, along with women, have been identified as the group experiencing the highest level of growth of HIV infection, the majority of infected teens are completely unaware of
their positive status. Convincing teenagers, or anyone else, to take
HIV antibody tests is an extremely difficult endeavor. Therefore, although the pool of infected youth is larger than we would like it to

be, the pool of *informed* infected youth is only a fraction of that. Also, because HIV-positive youth fear the threat of discrimination against them, many adolescents who know of their infection are unwilling to come forward. If teachers are able to find such youth who are also compelling speakers, they are highly advised to bring them in to talk to their classes. If they are not able to find HIV-positive heterosexual adolescents of similar ethnic makeup to their students, teachers are advised to locate capable speakers through local AIDS service organizations. A compelling HIV-positive speaker who differs from students is certainly better than no HIV-positive speaker at all.

Peer Education Programs

One way teachers can bring teenagers into the class to address their students is through Peer Education Programs (PEPs). Based on the idea that teenagers can be effective teachers to their peers on such uncomfortable subjects, Peer Education Programs have been organized across the country and throughout the world. The Peer Education Program of Los Angeles (PEP/LA), for instance, has established more than twenty offshoot programs in California and other states around the country and supports satellite organizations in Paris, Moscow, Budapest, Tel Aviv, Siberia, and Suriname. New York City is also home to a Peer Education Program, and the Hawaii Departments of Education and Health have instituted a Peer Education Program through the schools.

A Peer Education Program trains teenagers to teach their peers about HIV and AIDS. In areas where PEP is an extracurricular activity, these teens make public appearances before school classrooms, teen clubs and organizations, medical groups, church associations, and anywhere else teenagers might congregate to talk about the problems of HIV infection and AIDS. Most PEP organizations are multicultural and include adolescents of varying ages, so teachers can certainly arrange to have peer speakers similar to the age and ethnic makeup of their classes. Peer educators are quite effective in imparting necessary information about how adolescents can protect themselves from HIV infection, and so offer an engaging alternative to teachers uncomfortable with imparting the facts of AIDS. Information on how teachers can utilize PEP techniques to help their own students become peer educators will be discussed in an upcoming chapter.

One feature that PEP/LA includes in its presentations is the presence of someone infected with HIV or living with AIDS to also address the audience. Having such individuals on hand enables PEP/LA to gain all the benefits of HIV-positive speakers addressed above. In this way, PEP/LA gains the positive aspects of teenage speakers who can relate to the young audience as well as HIV-positive speakers who are able to give HIV and AIDS a human face to boost the audience's empathy, understanding, and acceptance of those infected with HIV or living with AIDS. PEP can give teachers the best of both worlds while imparting this life-saving information.

CONCLUSION

While the presentation of information is only the first element of a successful AIDS education unit, teachers should keep in mind that it may be vitally important to students in ways they may never be aware of. Although methods of helping students prevent AIDS have yet to be discussed, they may come too late for some students. Teachers should always remind students of the National AIDS Hotline, there to answer their questions twenty-four hours a day. If students are concerned about their own status of HIV infection or that of others close to them, they should not hesitate to call the hotline.

After being exposed to this material about HIV transmission, some students may have even more reason to believe they might be infected with HIV. As part of their presentation of the facts of HIV and AIDS, teachers should also stress the importance of HIV antibody testing. If students have any inkling that they may have been at risk for HIV infection, they should be urged to take this test. As is often the case with this topic, however, teachers will likely be unaware of a student's concern, so the message of testing must be promulgated to the entire class. If a student is infected with HIV, earlier testing to confirm it can provide greater treatment options and may result in a longer, richer life than ignoring the infection can possibly provide. Students must be convinced that they are better off knowing and addressing their infection than living in ignorance of it until it forces its way into their lives. An early negative test can put a student's mind at ease and end the worry. HIV antibody testing, whether with positive or negative results, can also bring home the seriousness of the AIDS pandemic. Going through the worry and speculation that accompanies waiting for an HIV status report can be a very sobering experience for students and can establish a common ground of empathy with those living with HIV infection or AIDS.

6

Skills to Change Student Attitudes Toward AIDS and Risky Behavior

It cannot be stated often enough that the ultimate goal of AIDS education is to influence students to avoid behaviors that put them at risk of HIV infection. Informing students of which behaviors are risky and which are safer lets them know the risks, but does nothing to motivate them to change their own actions. In order to actually affect student behaviors, teachers must first influence student attitudes.

This chapter will address methods by which teachers can influence their students' attitudes and behaviors through instructing them on healthy behavior, helping them to recognize problem situations in which risks might arise, and presenting them with skills to protect themselves in such situations. Behavior will not change until beliefs and attitudes about safer behavior have shifted toward a more accepting position. Teachers can influence what students believe about HIV risk behavior through such approaches as teaching refusal skills to help students understand, recognize, and avoid high-risk situations, and disseminating accurate peer group statistics so students can understand that accepted peer norms are often wildly inflated. Methods to reinforce these more positive student attitudes will be presented in the following chapter. Although some of these methods can be somewhat time-consuming, teachers will find that they have an excellent opportunity to truly affect their students' lives positively in ways that may actually save lives somewhere down the road.

AFFECTING BEHAVIOR THROUGH ATTITUDE

Human behavior is a very complicated matter. People, especially during their adolescence, do the things they do for a complex and often unfathomable number of different reasons. Sometimes the reasoning appears to make sense, sometimes it does not. The frustration in attempting to influence behavior change comes from there being no way, short of force, to make someone behave in a particular way. At best, teachers are only able to inspire a change in their students' beliefs or attitudes, but this may or may not inspire actual behavior modification. In initiating such a course of action in their classrooms, teachers must hold on to a certain amount of patience. Change can come, but it usually comes slowly. Just because immediate results are not apparent, teachers should not lose faith in the process.

The first step in addressing attitudes is to help students clarify their individual viewpoints toward and beliefs about sexuality and drug use. Although popular culture often implies that sexual activity occurs without consequence, anyone with any sexual experience at all realizes that this is not true. Teachers can help their students recognize and acknowledge that sexual partners often have differing objectives toward physical pleasure and emotional attachment when seeking sexual activity. If students understand and clarify what they want to achieve through sexual relations, whether that goal is physical pleasure, emotional sharing, a long-term loving relationship, or anything else, they will be in a better position to react responsibly when they experience sexual urges. The clichéd expectation of adolescent sexuality casts the sexually aroused male as a brute attempting to persuade the reluctant female to indulge his desires. Like all clichés, this has a some basis in truth, but it is not a hard-and-fast blueprint. Sometimes both partners are reluctant but feel social pressure to become sexually active. Males often believe that this clichéd response is expected of them, and attempt to feel out their way to their own level of comfort. Many females search for the thin line between appearing too eager for sex and fulfilling their own sexual desires. By introducing students to a breadth of viable attitudes and feelings concerning their sexual urges, teachers can help them realize that reactions to sexual situations need not be cast in stone, males responding in lusty lockstep while females collectively recoil in chaste reticence. Sexuality is one of the most personal subjects adolescents are likely to encounter, and they should be encouraged to accept their individual needs, desires, and emotions about it. The decisions they make concerning their sexual behavior can have many emotional and physical repercussions, HIV infection being the most dire. Attitude is an important factor in sexual decision-making and lays the groundwork for all that comes after. Clear attitudes can lead to clear decision-making.

Sexual decision-making, like decisions that must be reached in all areas, requires teenagers to become responsible. Growing up, unfortunately, is largely a matter of trial and error. Many of the decisions adolescents make about sexuality may be mistakes. Responsibility is a matter of attitude, and teachers can help their students learn to accept responsibility for their actions, whether they are based on good decisions or poor decisions. Adolescents who are willing to take responsibility for the things that they do are much more likely to examine their actions and take time to consider their choices. Educated students who have been exposed to and understand the full range of choices available to them will be in a much stronger position to assume responsibility for their actions than students who have not. Practice in making decisions through methods explored later in this chapter can help students learn how to assume an attitude of responsibility.

Accurate Adolescent Sexual Norms

One method of helping adolescents free themselves of the herd mentality that generally surrounds sexuality is to clarify the actual levels of peer sexual activity. Unlike adults, who often ignore or underestimate the level of adolescent sexual activity, teenagers can wildly exaggerate it. Many teens assume that everybody else is already sexually active while they sit alone, falling behind in their maturation process. As we have seen previously, the norm for adolescent sexuality is considerably lower than the one hundred percent many teens expect it to be. It is not until ages nineteen and twenty that the level of sexual activity for males and females rises above seventy-five percent. For younger adolescents of thirteen, fourteen, or fifteen, the level of sexual activity is considerably lower. This information, correcting the mistaken belief that the majority of young adolescents have already become sexually active, can be very comforting to teens who remain uncomfortable about pursuing such activity but want to keep up with what they believe their friends are doing. If the true norm of adolescent sexual activity is promoted by teachers, the perceived peer pressure teens exert on each other to become sexually active can be diminished. The inflated expectations of teen sexual activity can be corrected, and peer pressure can be modified to reflect the true feelings that most teens possess.

Building Self-Esteem

Teachers can also undermine adolescent peer pressure by encouraging their students to build their personal levels of self-esteem and self-confidence. If students possess a strong sense of self, they are less likely to fall into line behind perceived peer expectations. Apart from the other benefits students might receive from self-esteem, it has also been tied to the avoidance of unprotected sex among teenage males.[1] Teens who feel and project self-confidence are able to act independently of their peers, accept responsibility for their actions and decisions, and exhibit a sense of pride in their own accomplishments. Teachers can stimulate self-confidence among their students by presenting their AIDS-prevention material in small steps, which will allow students to master it. If teachers allow themselves to be overwhelmed by what seems like a large amount of information to be disseminated in a small amount of time, and inundate their students with too much too quickly, students will become frustrated, will stop paying attention, and will learn little or nothing about HIV and AIDS. If, however, teachers can encourage their students by teaching the material clearly, concisely, and understandably, students will begin to feel more sure of their ability to practice the protective techniques, and thus build self-esteem and self-confidence.

Another method of strengthening confidence among students is to focus on any goals they may have for the future. Teachers can help them recognize or create challenging yet realistic goals, giving them a reason to protect themselves from health threats they may encounter in the present. Adolescents who have the self-esteem and self-confidence necessary to push themselves forward toward future ambitions will develop the presence of mind to protect themselves from HIV infection. Anything teachers can do to promote high self-esteem among their students will pay off.

For and Against

For and Against is an activity that can help students recognize and alter their attitudes about sexual activity and the possibility of contracting HIV. As opposed to other subjects we will discuss later in this chapter, For and Against is primarily knowledge-based. In this activity, teachers identify a behavior that can reduce the risk of HIV transmission, and students give reasons why the behavior is easy or difficult to practice. One such behavior might be to abstain from drinking alcohol at a party. The teacher will ask students why it might be difficult to abstain from drinking. Students might come up with answers such as "Everyone else is drinking," "I like the feeling that comes from drinking," "Drinking helps put me at ease," and others. One student should stand at the board, making a list of these reasons, or excuses, for drinking. After students have had an opportunity to think through why it is difficult to avoid drinking, the arguments against risk-reduction behavior, they should start a new list detailing reasons to practice the risk-reduction behavior. These might include answers such as "I can keep a clear head," "It's easier to remember to practice safe sex when you're not drunk," and "I make better decisions without alcohol." If adolescents are able to think through the implications and consequences of high-risk behavior and puzzle out some possible ways of avoiding it while sitting in the safety of the classroom, they will be in a much better position to make the decision for low-risk behavior when it really counts, in the midst of the high-pressure situation itself. The reasoning process will be behind them, and students will be able to fall into the habit of making safer, lower-risk responses.

REFUSAL SKILLS

Simply knowing the correct safe responses and behaviors, as we have already seen, does not give adolescents enough power to follow through to practice those behaviors. They must also know how to implement and support safe behavior. They must practice the skills they will need to utilize in making the best decisions and following through on low-risk behaviors. Identifying and practicing refusal skills will be an important part of any successful AIDS education program.

No matter how high students might score on knowledge tests about HIV and AIDS, or even on tests asking for reasons why they should practice abstinence or protective sex, making decisions and sticking with them becomes much more difficult in the midst of a risk situation. This predicament is similar to what would happen if teachers and parents told students that they must, under all circumstances, be sure to keep their checkbooks balanced and yet neglect to teach them simple addition and subtraction skills. Teachers and parents could make sure students understood that, without regular balancing, checking accounts can easily be overspent and overdrawn. Students might even be able to explain back to their parents that the results of an unbalanced checkbook can be overdrafts and bounced checks. However, without the simple math skills necessary to add new deposits and subtract checks and other withdrawals, students have no choice but to watch their checking account become exhausted, all the while expecting the dire consequences they have been warned against.

Behavioral skills to help adolescents avoid high-risk situations perform precisely the same function in regard to keeping students safe from HIV, AIDS, and other dangers. In the backseat of a car, with a highly desirable partner, adolescents are faced with the same danger for HIV infection that they would face for a bounced check when attempting to buy a new portable CD player with an empty bank account. Fortunately, just as they can teach addition and subtraction, teachers can help their students develop the skills to recognize risky situations, make and keep to the most effective decision to avoid those situations, and negotiate themselves out of risky situations if recognition comes too late.

Failure to provide students with a method of modifying their behavior to reduce their risk of contracting AIDS can leave them feeling frustrated, helpless, and fatalistic. What is worse, they will continue to pursue their old habits and ways of behavior, leaving any hope for behavior modification by the wayside. Any AIDS education program that has any hope for success will need to spend a substantial amount of time on behavioral skills. Holding to our established fifteen-hour minimum for program effectiveness, as many as eleven or twelve hours should be assigned to the various refusal skills. An effective AIDS education curriculum will be measured in its students' success in avoiding risk behaviors, an eventuality that can only be achieved through extensive practice and rehearsal of refusal skills. After the successful completion of the AIDS unit, teachers will also want to return from time to time to the skills material in order to refresh their students' memories and sharpen their students' practice of these skills.

One of the most difficult tasks teachers might find in delivering instruction of refusal skills is to keep the subject matter very specific. Romantic and sexual behavior has always been shrouded in metaphor and euphemism, and teachers may find that their instinct is to continue this practice. Such a turn of events, however, will prove disastrous in attempting to furnish students with these necessary skills. A metaphor can only be effective when all parties understand its meaning. Adolescents who have had only limited experience with sexual situations and have been exposed to sexual information through rumor and innuendo do not have clear ideas of the concepts and activities that teachers must address in this unit. Refusal skills must be practical and specific. Once children become adolescents, discussing unwanted sexual activities in terms of "someone touching you in such a way that you become uncomfortable" will not carry the necessary weight to enable adolescents to recognize high-risk situations before they arise. Teachers must talk quite specifically about how students might handle situations in which both partners want to have sexual intercourse but do not have convenient protection available, situations that appear to start out safely enough but quickly escalate to a level of discomfort when one partner insists on becoming more sexually involved than the other partner desires, situations that are immediately uncomfortable and present the possibility of forced or otherwise coerced sexual activity, and any other situations that teachers or students can imagine.

It should go without saying that, even more so than during the fact- and information-based components, a nonjudgmental classroom environment is vital to the successful treatment of this material. Sexual material is uncomfortable to some degree because it is kept undercover and is rarely addressed in "respectable" public forums. Some students, therefore, may be reticent to talk openly about these situations. If they fear ridicule or rejection, they will become even more reluctant to accept and consider the material offered by the teacher. Teachers trying to engage unresponsive students who blankly sit through the AIDS education unit will

ultimately serve no one. Students will not incorporate the potentially life-saving refusal skills into their behavior, and teachers will
become frustrated by the level of energy such material demands ex-
pended for no obvious reason. The classroom must become as open,
accepting, and nonjudgmental as possible in order to appeal to students and bring them into the discussion and activity. During the
practice of refusal skills, many students will try to create their own
methods of refusal and put a personal spin on those presented by
teachers or other students. Such creative endeavors will quickly dry
up if students fear reprisal or scorn if they fail. Teachers must do
everything in their power to provide an environment of acceptance
and approval for their students.

Ten Refusal Skills

Educational programs that have successfully utilized refusal skills
have generally addressed the abuse of substances such as drugs, alcohol, and tobacco.[2] Substance abuse lends itself to a "Just Say No"
approach much more readily than do sexual situations. As we have
already explored, "no" is not always the appropriate response to
every possibility of sexual activity. Refusal skills for sexual responsibility, therefore, require more thought and more attention to the individual's expectations and desires than similar skills programs that
depend on repetition and rote to refuse a drink or a cigarette. Where
the appropriate conclusion to a drug or alcohol situation is relatively
easy to identify, sexual situations demand more consideration.
Sometimes the best resolution is to completely escape the predicament. At other times, however, individuals may want to pursue the
sexual opportunity to some extent, perhaps even to an act of protected intercourse. Every sexual situation is unique and requires a
unique decision-making process. The skills listed and defined here
reflect a very conscious process of thought, observation, and awareness that students will need to employ in making responsible decisions when faced with sexual activity. Once a decision is made, fol-
low-up skills will help students carry out that decision, whether it is
to keep themselves clear of risky situations or to navigate themselves
through them safely.

Sexual decision-making and refusal skills can also be extended
to include situations involving substance abuse. Students are being
taught to make responsible decisions, and responsible decision-making is the backbone of refusing alcohol, tobacco, and drugs. Students

trained in these sexual refusal skills will be in a position to keep themselves out of a wide variety of high-risk situations.

1   Talking to Myself. This is the most basic refusal skill, and the foundation of all that follow.   Students are encouraged to consciously talk to themselves, aloud if necessary, to remind themselves of their feelings and desires concerning particular situations. Through talking to ourselves, we can give ourselves encouragement and sometimes puzzle out problems.   Not all sexual situations arise unexpectedly, of course.   When students plan a date or other type of outing with members of the opposite sex, they often have hopes and intentions of what will happen.   A girl preparing for an evening of studying with her boyfriend may plan how to turn the evening toward kissing, petting, and other foreplay.   If she does not want to follow through all the way to intercourse, she should prepare a similar plan of how to slow her boyfriend down if he attempts to push the experience further.   No one, male or female, should ever be surprised if kissing and cuddling begin to take a more serious turn.

Talking to Myself will help adolescents preparing for a date or other event to set limits on their behavior ahead of time.   It will also help them stick to those limits during sexual activity.   While getting dressed, for instance, an adolescent might say, "I want each of us to keep our clothes on and keep all touching above the waist."   This can be done either silently or aloud. Some teens even find that stating it to themselves in front of a mirror is helpful.   After a limit has been set, adolescents should continue to talk to themselves as a way of offering encouragement: "I am capable of remaining in control of myself and my partner"; "I've made my decision, and I'm going to stick to it"; or "I know the right thing to do, and I can do it."   Talking to Myself gives teens a sense of their own powers and abilities in making good decisions and keeping them on track.

Sometimes, however, no matter how prepared someone feels, physical urges can overtake intellectual decisions regarding a sexual situation or encounter.   Adolescents may want to backpedal on the limits they had already set.   By talking to themselves during the encounter, however, they can reassert those limits. Talking to themselves enables people to stop, emotionally remove themselves from the present moment a little bit, and reattain control.   Teens can start with simple statements such as "Wait a minute," or "Hold on."   Once they've gained their own attention, they might say things to themselves such as: "This feels good now, but I know I'll be sorry later"; "I already made a decision not to get too involved"; or "I respect myself too much to let this continue." Talking to Myself, as simple as it sounds, can actually become a person's most powerful weapon in keeping situations under control.

2   Listening to Myself. Although this sounds like an obvious extension of Talking to Myself, Listening to Myself actually stands alone as a complementary skill. Teachers and many students understand that it does not matter how much someone talks if no one is listening. Every conversation needs two participants, a speaker and a listener. When using the skill of Listening to Myself, students will find that they must pay attention to their Talking to Myself statements. It is useless for people to say "I know I can do this" if they refuse to listen and believe. Often individuals have conversations in their minds in which they disagree with themselves, one part of their mind offering encouragement, while another part undermines them. Instead of ignoring a self-statement such as "I can control myself," students must hear and accept this statement as true.

Listening to Myself incorporates other functions as well. Often people ignore or refuse to acknowledge their feelings and instincts. Some people experience worry as a tight feeling in the pit of their stomachs. A common, if impractical reaction to this sensation is to push the feeling down and try to make it go away. Instead of solving the problem, this reaction forces the worry to make itself known through other sensations, such as nervousness, stammering, sweaty palms, or unclear thinking. Other feelings that cause physical reactions are fear, happiness, sadness, embarrassment, excitement, and frustration. By using the technique of listening to themselves, people can acknowledge what they are feeling and seek an explanation to it or do something about it. What has happened or is happening to cause this feeling? Students might realize that they are worried because they face a challenging test, that they are happy because they made the track team, or that they are embarrassed because they unexpectedly ran into someone they have a crush on. Just understanding their feelings can help bring some relief to the sensations, and in some cases recognizing and identifying the feeling can lead to addressing it. Students worried about a test can alleviate some of that worry by studying. People scared of entering a particular neighborhood can avoid that neighborhood. Many adolescents' feelings are not as easy to figure out and respond to as these examples, but they can be addressed in exactly the same way.

Listening to Myself can be most helpful in confusing situations when emotions and feelings are less than obvious. This often occurs during high-risk situations. Fear and anxiety can be present when a person is faced with the prospect of having to turn down an offer of drugs from a friend. Feelings of desire, lust, and love are often, though not always, present during sexual situations. When they are present, they can offer a fair bit of confusion to adolescents trying to hold on to their preset limits. An adolescent might think, "I decided before that I would not do more than this, but I sure feel like going farther now." It is certainly possible that adolescents may set their sexual limits and then decide to change them in midcourse. Such a decision would not be reasoned and well-thought-out, so it may not be a good one. Decisions such as this made under poor circumstances are often decisions that people regret later. If students are aware of the cravings and desires that result from sexual situations, they can listen to themselves, recognize these feelings when they occur, and prevent themselves from being fooled into going further sexually than they would prefer. That is the point where students go back to Skill Number1 and begin to talk to themselves about their previously set limits.

3   Setting Limits. This is perhaps the most personal refusal skill, because everyone has his or her own levels of confidence, comfort, and ability, and these are the factors that must determine the limits we each set. No one can set limits for anyone else; we must each set our own.

The limits that individuals set on sexual situations must be firm and specific. Many teens simply want to set as a limit something like: "I will not do anything to make myself uncomfortable." While this may sound fine on the surface, it has problems because no one can always judge what will make them uncomfortable until after the fact. Limits must be preset so that adolescents will protect themselves from risky and uncomfortable situations before they ever arise. If a limit is constant and firm, it will always be in place when it is needed.

Some students may suggest that their limits should differ in separate situations. This is another idea which may sound good on its surface but which cannot stand up to scrutiny. A limit should be the maximum amount that an individual is willing to accept of any activity. One example of this concept is the volume of a stereo system that can rise to a volume of 10. Some speakers can only withstand so much wattage, or volume, before they become overloaded and blow out. If there is danger that an adolescent's stereo speakers will be blown out when the volume is turned up louder than 7, then 7 would be the constant and firm limit. Under no circumstances will the adolescent turn the stereo louder than 7. When that adolescent's mother is at home, however, she might not like the stereo to go louder than 4. This is not a case of two different limits, one with the mother and one without. There is only one limit, 7, and the stereo is never turned louder than that. However, there will be times, such as when the mother is home, when the adolescent chooses to stop before reaching the limit.

This idea can be transferred to a sexual context if we take a teenage girl, Maria, as an example. Maria may decide that when she is in a sexual situation, she will let her boyfriend, Zack, put his hands into and under her shirt, but she will never take her shirt off or let Zack take her shirt off. This is her constant and firm limit. However, just because she might go this far sometimes does not mean that she will go this far every time. She might go out with Jim one night and decide to go no further than kissing. Another time she might be with Chris and not even kiss him at all. But under no circumstances, with no particular boyfriend, will Maria take off her shirt.

Setting limits can be a very tricky endeavor. Because they should ideally be set before an individual encounters a risk situation, that person may not always know precisely where to set the limit. To set limits most effectively, students should return to Skill Number 2, Listening to Myself. By identifying and then considering their feelings about their values and about sexuality, adolescents can discover their areas of comfort and discomfort fairly accurately. They can think about what makes them feel awkward, embarrassed, or uncomfortable. They can also think about activities that make them feel wanted, desirable, and happy. Students develop their sexuality at different levels. Within one class, teachers might find a few students who are comfortable in some situations with intercourse, other students who are comfortable with nudity but not with intercourse, others who would never consider nudity but enjoy heavy kissing and fondling, and still others who are most comfortable simply talking with a romantic partner. Because students will not be sharing their limits with their friends, they need not succumb to peer influence. Teachers should attempt to establish that, in setting personal limits, there is no overriding right or wrong answer. Each individual will have limits that are right for him or her, but no two students will necessarily agree on their limits.

Teachers can most help their students set limits by making sure that students recognize and understand the repercussions of the various decisions they might make. If, for instance, students are prepared to set their sexual limit at intercourse, teachers should do what they can to encourage them to make a commitment to condoms as part of that limit. Unfortunately, this is more difficult than it looks, because students will be setting their limits privately. Some teachers might think it is a good idea to have students write down their limits and turn them in as an assignment. While encouraging students to write down their limits as a sort of private commitment to themselves, asking them to make their limits known to each other or to the teacher will just result in a high level of disingenuousness among the students. If a student intends to pursue intercourse, he or she will not become vulnerable to a teacher's disapproval by announcing it. Instead, this student is much more likely to write down a more innocuous limit and allow the teacher to assume that he or she is teaching a class full of virgins. Because teachers will not know their students' chosen limits and will be unable to counsel each student, they must be sure that they have thoroughly covered the informational material discussed earlier. A student's commitment to unfailingly wear a condom during high-risk sexual activity is infinitely preferable to no limit on sexual activity at all.

4   Recognizing a Risk Situation.   Of all the skills listed here, Recognizing a Risk Situation may be the most difficult to teach. Basically, this skill rests in common sense, which is a difficult quality to impart to others. A good start, however, might be to choose obvious risk situations as examples and work down from there. If a particular house in the neighborhood is a notorious crack house and sometimes the site of drive-by shootings, virtually everyone will recognize this as a possible risk situation and go out of their way to avoid it. A more innocuous example might be the crosstown rival's football locker room after your team has just won the city championship. These football players would be in no mood to see cheering fans from the winning team. When teachers describe these or other examples, their students will likely have some sort of visceral reaction to them. It might be a tightening of the stomach, a catch in the throat, or something else. Teachers should guide students back to Skill Number 2, Listening to Myself, to determine what emotions they are feeling. Obvious choices might be fear and anxiety, but students should be allowed to identify their own feelings. They will learn that their bodies can be relied on to identify risk situations. When people face danger, whether it is physical or emotional, their bodies usually make it known to them.

To make it clear that risk situations are not always as obvious as these examples, teachers might introduce a few more common examples. Students may feel similar physical sensations when approaching the classroom for a final exam. Likewise, some students who have jobs may have felt anxiety on their first day. There are a wide variety of risk situations that adolescents experience. Some may have valid physical danger associated with them, while others might involve social and emotional perils. As we can see through the preceding examples, not all risk situations should be automatically avoided. Ducking out of a final exam, for example, can introduce a situation of much greater risk than that involved in simply taking the test.

As students gain more and more experience with risk situations and with life in general, they may develop more common sense that can help them identify risk situations even before their bodies begin their warning processes. They will also begin to recognize that not all physical sensations are warnings of risk. The sensations associated with excitement, for example, can often be mistaken for anxiety. Experience will help adolescents begin to differentiate between the two. Likewise, experience will also help adolescents recognize and address different types of risk situations. Some risk situations are easily solved, such as simply avoiding the street where the crack house is. Other risk situations, however, may require more complicated resolutions As students accumulate more experience, they will be better able to solve or avoid such situations, but if they are well grounded in Recognizing a Risk Situation, they will have conquered the first step in that process.

5   Making a Decision. This is the skill that requires the most conscious thinking on the part of students. Most of our previous skills have demanded that students pay attention to their surroundings or their feelings, recognizing what is going on in and around them. Now, however, we must assume that students have gathered all the information they need to make a good decision. They recognize and understand the risk they face (Skill Number 4), their feelings about the risk (Skill Number 2), and the limits they have set to deal with the risk (Skill Number 3). In order to make an appropriate decision, students should consider all the information available to them, weighing its strengths and its weaknesses. After reviewing each of the solutions to a risk situation, students will then choose the best and act upon it.

In any particular situation, a number of potential solutions will be available to students. To once again take up our example of a crack house that students must pass to walk home, teens who search will find a number of viable resolutions. One possibility is simply to walk around the block, avoiding the street in front of the house. Perhaps a different route home can take students past a convenience store, which could provide a candy bar as a reward for avoiding the risk situation. Another possibility is to get a ride from a parent, sibling, or friend. Upon closer examination, students may find that at some times of the day it is relatively safe to pass by the house. After gathering a number of possible solutions, students can weigh the pluses and minuses of each and decide upon the best.

It is best to begin the decision-making process before one is face-to-face with a risk situation. If a student waits until he is approaching the crack house to decide how to escape the risk, his potential options are quite limited, perhaps consisting only of walking around the block. If, on the other hand, he considered the decision before leaving school, he would have a broader range of possibilities from which to choose. On one particular day, this student has no money, so he could not reward himself with a candy bar after taking an alternate route. The student's older sister has a car, but she also has a meeting after school, so he would have to wait for half an hour before getting a ride home. The student could walk home, going around the block to avoid the crack house, but this still makes him somewhat nervous. Of these choices, he decides that waiting for his older sister is the best solution. While he is waiting, he can even do a homework assignment, thus making good use of his time.

Unfortunately, not all decisions are as clear-cut as this example. Some decisions to avoid risk situations demand that students avoid or refuse their friends. Others may allow only a selection of less-than-desirable alternatives. Adolescents may also find themselves from time to time in an unexpected risk situation that does not allow a lot of time to carefully identify and weigh each of the options. In such a predicament, perhaps a single avenue of escape will be recognized and followed. Upon consideration later, an individual might realize that other, better options were available, but the most important point is that the risk situation was avoided. Even in a panic situation, all decision-making follows the same process, whether relaxed or rushed. In an unexpected, confusing situation, previous practice will greatly enhance an adolescent's ability to make a responsible decision.

As an example, we can again refer to Maria, the teenager who decided to set her limit at never removing her shirt in a sexual situation. She and her boyfriend Zack may be sitting on the couch kissing and fondling each other when he starts to take her shirt off. Maria may or may not have expected this, but she must quickly make a decision to hold to her constant and firm limit or to break it. Because she had put a lot of time and consideration into setting her limit in the first place, she knows that going past it would make her uncomfortable. In fact, if Maria listens to herself, she might find that she already is feeling anxious about the situation. By talking to herself, Maria can remind herself of her limit and encourage herself to hold to it. She can quickly make the decision that she will not allow Zack to remove her shirt and then take steps to remain in control.

Although students may find that Making a Decision and standing up for it can sometimes feel awkward, they will learn that, with practice, it will ultimately begin to come more easily. Other skills described below will also offer aid in making the decision stick.

6   Giving No for an Answer. The skills we have been discussing are refusal skills, so it is only natural that we should come to the most basic refusal skill of all: saying no. Although this skill is only a step beyond Making a Decision, it is the crux of the entire skills curriculum. It does not matter that students know the right thing if they cannot do the right thing.

Giving No for an Answer sounds simple enough, but anyone who has ever expressed an unpopular view in an awkward situation knows that it is very easy to compromise on their feelings and convictions. Because this curriculum is aimed primarily at protecting students from AIDS, whether that means refusing unwanted sexual activity or avoiding undesirable drug use, students are being asked to give no for an answer in what are likely to be emotionally charged situations. Many students will not be able to simply say, "No, I'd rather not do that" and have the issue dropped. They will have to be firm and sure in their statements.

In fact, firmness is the strongest weapon that students can use when saying no. They can repeat the word no several times, making it clear that this is not a temporary hesitation. The more assertive someone sounds when saying no, the more he or she will be believed. Assertiveness can be strengthened if students are able to make their point in firm, complete sentences that address their partner and state their feelings, such as "No, I don't want you to do that" or "This makes me uncomfortable, so please stop." Statements that assertively use the pronouns "I" and "you" will be more persuasive than simply saying no.

Unfortunately, the word no has come to be misunderstood in sexual situations. We have all heard the cliché that women make all the decisions and set all the limits in sexual activity. It is believed by many that the man will keep pushing the level of activity until the woman stops him. A corollary to this cliché is that "good" women cannot be seen to enjoy sexual activity, so they can never actively agree to it. Therefore, the idea has spread that a woman's "no" means "maybe," while "maybe" means "yes." This system of communication, unfortunately, leaves us without a word to mean "no." In view of this cliché, one partner lightly saying "no" may not convince the other partner to stop. There can be little ambiguity, however, in a statement such as "I told you to stop."

Nonverbal responses can also be used effectively for students to get their message across. Looking someone in the eye is a good way for adolescents to indicate that they are serious. If adolescents flinch or look away, their partners may think there is a possible avenue around the refusal. When partners are sitting together, perhaps with their arms intertwined, the refusing partner can sit up to establish upright posture as part of the refusal process. If the partners are standing, posture can be even more effective if the refusing partner stands with shoulders back and chest out.

Some students, fearing that rejection might drive their friends away, may have trouble taking responsibility for a negative response. If this is a problem, they can simply blame someone else. Parents are always a good target at which to point blame. A less secure adolescent might say, "My parents are coming to pick me up soon, and if they find us like this, they'll kill me." Because the most important issue here is that such students indeed say no when they need to, if shifting responsibility allows them to do that, then they should by all means do so. The partner will not be alienated, but the high-risk activity will stop. Most parents will be more than happy to accept the label of "bad guy" if it helps their children.

Giving No for an Answer in a sexual situation can sometimes be quite easy. Students will most likely want to say "no" when they are approaching their constant and firm preset limit. On the printed page, this seems like an abstract, intellectual idea. In a real situation, however, it is likely to be very emotional. Students have chosen their limits after a great deal of thought and reflection, considering what makes them comfortable and what makes them uncomfortable. An adolescent whose sexual limit is challenged will not coolly and calmly suggest that his or her partner stop. The approaching activity is something that the adolescent has definitely decided he or she does not want to do, and all the physical and emotional feelings that were explored during the Listening to Myself skill will resurface. Most students will not have to remind themselves of where their limits are.

7   Offering Alternatives.   One assumption of providing students with skills to avoid high-risk situations and behaviors is that each student does not live in a vacuum. So far we have only discussed how students can assert themselves to refuse the advances of others. Unfortunately, not everyone is easily refused. In sexual situations, some people see refusal as a challenge, and press their desire even harder. Students must be prepared to offer alternate suggestions if they hope to defuse a potentially explosive situation.

Because every student will have set his or her own limits, he or she will also have to explore and identify individual alternatives. Teachers might, however, offer a few examples of how people with particular limits might offer alternatives. For instance, if a student has set his limit at kissing and fondling, he would be uncomfortable if his partner began to undress. Therefore, he might suggest holding tightly, kissing, or putting off the nudity until a later time. If his partner balks, he can simply explain that he is uncomfortable with the way events are unfolding. Most partners will not take this as rejection but will be glad to accommodate the other's wishes and continue the encounter. A more stern refusal will only be necessary if his partner insists on undressing. Another student may have decided that she can accept nudity but she does not want to have intercourse. She and her partner are lying together naked when he initiates intercourse. She can stop him and suggest that they share intimate kissing and touching, instead. By acknowledging her partner's desires yet refusing them, she can explain her feelings and why she has chosen to stop where she has. Again, only if her partner insists on following through with the intercourse he has initiated must she become more firm.

Offering alternatives once an activity has been initiated, however, can be somewhat awkward. A better alternative is for partners to discuss their limits ahead of time. This might not be practical for teens on a first date who are not yet comfortable with each other on that level, but it is certainly possible for a couple who has been seeing each other for some time. If limits are set ahead of time, there will be no misunderstanding or hurt feelings caused by rejection when the limits are approached. A couple may even learn that each partner has similar limits and avoid much of the worry and anxiety that go with risky sexual situations. Agreed-upon limits set at the beginning of an evening can make the entire dating experience less stressful. In a way, this is like extending Skill Number 1, Talking to Myself, to two people rather than an individual.

Offering Alternatives is a useful strategy for more than sexual situations. If a student is going out with a group of her friends who, she worries, have been getting into trouble, she can suggest that instead of driving around aimlessly, they all go to a movie. Likewise, another student might go to a football game with his friends. He knows that for the last two weeks, these same friends have been getting into fights in the parking lot after the game. Instead of standing around waiting for trouble, however, he might suggest that they go and grab a pizza. Offering Alternatives is a skill that students can use throughout their lives to avoid risky situations.

8   Protecting Myself in a Risk Situation. This skill is most useful when students recognize a risk situation that they may be unable to avoid. If students are entering or have already entered a risk situation that they cannot or do not wish to leave, they can take steps to protect themselves from the greatest harm.

The first, most obvious function this skill can serve is to provide teenagers with a position from which to negotiate condom use during intercourse. To state the obvious, partners engaged in mutually desired intercourse are not always in agreement over the use of condoms. Many times, one partner wishes the protection of condoms while the other partner does not want to bother with them. Instead of falling back on the argument of condoms or nothing or giving in to a partner's pressure to have unprotected intercourse, there is a third course: negotiation. Condom negotiation is most successful when it occurs before any sexual involvement, so that both partners can properly prepare themselves for condom use. If one partner only raises the issue of condoms after a period of foreplay and just before intercourse, that partner will be at a definite disadvantage. Physical urges and desires can be overwhelming, and trying to stop them in order to change the rules of the encounter at the last minute can be very difficult.

To begin condom negotiation, the partner desiring to use condoms should make his or her feelings on the issue clear. Most people have thought about this issue quite a bit before they raise it in conversation, so they have had a lot of time to practice Skill Number 2, Listening to Myself. The feelings discovered during this process should be shared with a partner, who may respond favorably to them. If the partner does not immediately respond in this way, the adolescent must then try reason as a way to convince the partner. This incorporates skills of articulating feelings and listening to the partner's feelings. An adolescent might express feelings of fear of personal infection or possible pregnancy as a result of the intercourse, as well as a desire to protect both partners against HIV, other STDs, and pregnancy. After making his or her own feelings clear, the adolescent should take the opportunity to listen to those of the partner. Even if the partner disagrees and wants to have unprotected intercourse, by bringing the issue out into the open, the couple may find a middle ground for agreement and compromise. Compromise is, of course, a precarious word to use in this situation. Some compromises may be possible, but adolescents should not compromise on the basic issue of condoms themselves. Compromising and agreeing to use condoms half the time and no condoms the other half ultimately leaves both partners vulnerable to disease and pregnancy. One possible compromise is to follow through with the planned intercourse. If a partner is unwilling to use condoms, a student should refuse to engage in intercourse at all. No student should set any limit farther than protected intercourse, so intercourse without condoms should be off limits for everyone. As an alternative to no intercourse, protected intercourse itself can be a compromise.

During condom negotiation, the partner desiring unprotected sex may offer compelling and convincing arguments for why condoms are unnecessary. Many males and some females maintain that condoms take all the sensation, and therefore all the pleasure, from intercourse. The classic no condom line, of course, is "If you loved and trusted me, you wouldn't ask me to use one." Students should listen to their partner's arguments and consider them. However, they should also use Skills Number 1 and Number 2 to talk to themselves and listen to themselves. Using Skill Number 1, students can remind themselves why they want to use condoms. Using Skill Number 2, they can examine their feelings and remember how uncomfortable they feel about unprotected sex. A compromise to the first argument that condoms make intercourse less pleasurable might be to find other ways to increase the pleasure. Some condoms feel less intrusive than others, and lubricants can sometimes provide greater sensation. Other condoms offer additional features, such as color or flavor, to spice up the encounter. Condoms can be made a part of foreplay, and even the act of putting a condom on can be eroticized, making it pleasurable for both partners.

The challenge put forward by the "if you loved me" statement can easily be put on its head and turned around against the partner who used it. A student who is confronted by this idea merely needs to ask his or her partner about love. If the partner "really loved" the student who has set limits, then that partner would not pressure the student to go against his or her personal limits. The test of love goes both ways. If partners really love each other, then they each want what is best for the other. A true love partner will not force the other into positions or activities that they both might regret later. The challenge of love does not only rest with the partner desiring unprotected sex.

These examples of negotiation and compromise, of course, can be adapted to any sexual limit that students may set. We have been discussing the most extreme example because it carries the highest risk. As much negotiation as possible should be conducted before the start of any activity, and adolescents should consider the implications of the possible compromises they may make before that discussion begins. If circumstances develop differently than adolescents expect, they may need to negotiate while they fend off an amorous partner. The most important thing for them to accomplish in such cases is to limit their risk as much as possible. If negotiation, compromise, and alternatives fail to convince a partner, the adolescent may have to fall back on Skill Number 6, Giving No for an Answer, and firmly refuse to take part in the activity any longer. Teens have the strength and ability to protect themselves when they have the confidence necessary to succeed.

Protecting Myself in a Risk Situation need not merely be limited to mutually desirable sexual encounters. Students will find themselves on the edges of many different types of situations that encourage risk behaviors. Too much drinking at a party, hanging with the wrong people, or going to a known drug location are activities that can each lead to risky behaviors. The best solution, of course, is to avoid and ignore such situations as much as possible, but that is not always an option. Sometimes adolescents might find that a risk is already in place before they even recognize it. It occasionally happens that friends will trick an adolescent into a tempting risk situation. When this happens, the most important action students can take to protect themselves is to keep their minds clear and their wits about them. Teens do not need to follow their friends mindlessly wherever they go. Students can be present at a risk situation but still remain aloof from it and refuse to participate. If necessary, watching as friends put themselves at risk is preferable to students doing it themselves. Everyone has a personal set of standards and limits, and they must be encouraged to stay true to them. Talking to Myself and Listening to Myself are both important components of Protecting Myself in a Risk Situation, and if students can master them, they will be in a good position to negotiate with others and keep themselves out of trouble and risk situations.

9   Leaving a Risk Situation. After an adolescent has exhausted Skill Number 8, he or she may be left with no other alternative than to leave the risk situation. In a way, this skill is only an extension of Skill Number 6, Giving No for an Answer. Like that skill, Leaving a Risk Situation depends largely on firmness.

Some situations may not allow students to protect themselves. Incidents of molestation or forced intimacy often involve a stronger person with whom negotiation will be pointless. After employing

Skill Number 4, Recognizing a Risk Situation, if students fail at Skill Number 8 and cannot protect themselves within the situation, they should do all they can to get away from it.

Feelings that might precede such a realization are fear and dread. Adolescents can count on these feelings to alert them to any danger they might face. In fact, these are emotions that usually run so strongly that adolescents experiencing them will not need to take time to listen to themselves--the feelings will virtually scream out their presence. Making a decision to leave will not be difficult; it may be the only decision adolescents feel they have available to them.

Defiantly walking away from a risk situation is not always the best solution. Before forcing some sort of confrontation, students can try to negotiate with their companions about leaving. If a student attends a party with a group of friends only to discover that he or she is quite uncomfortable there, for instance, the first attempt to leave should be made as a suggestion to the friends: "This isn't so much fun after all. Let's get out of here." Not all the friends will necessarily want to leave immediately, so some negotiation, as discussed in Skill Number 8, might be called for. Students can explain why they want to leave, or they can fall back on Skill Number 7 and suggest other activities everyone can enjoy together. In many instances, this will be enough to defuse a risk situation.

Unfortunately, simple persuasion is not always sufficient to end a risk situation. Some difficulties, such as sexual situations or drug solicitations, will involve only one other person who eagerly wants to continue. After negotiation and persuasion have failed, stronger measures, possibly including walking away alone, are necessary. Once students have completed Skill Number 5, Making a Decision, and decided that the only option left to them is to leave, they should be as firm as possible. Students should stop whatever they may be doing, stand up tall, look their companion or companions directly in the eye, and announce, "I don't want to do this. I'm leaving." Instead of waiting for a response, students should turn and walk away. Their companions may indeed try to stop them or talk them into staying, but, the decision already made, students should not stop to listen or argue. To engage in argument or persuasion at this point is to reopen the question of whether or not the students will stay. Instead of trying to work out a compromise at this time, students must remain firm and leave.

Leaving a risk situation can sometimes raise logistical problems. If a student who needs to leave such a predicament does not have his or her own car, if he or she came with a companion who does not intend to leave, then the student will need to walk away and find some sort of transportation. Perhaps the student can catch a bus home or walk to a fast food restaurant or convenience store to call home for a ride or even call a cab. This is much preferable to remaining at risk. Students should always try to carry enough money to cover any unexpected expenses such as these.

Likewise, the student who decides to leave the risk situation may have the only car available and may have given everyone else a ride. Too bad. If the situation is dangerous enough to warrant leaving, students cannot continue to expose themselves to risk so that their friends can have a ride home. If friends needing a ride do not want to leave with the students who are protecting themselves from risk, then they are on their own and can find their own ride home. It is not the responsibility of any students to provide transportation for others by putting themselves at risk.

Because emotions often run high in risk situations such as unwanted sexual activity or drug promotions, defiantly walking away is not always a viable option for students. Attempting to leave a risk situation can sometimes lead to fights or other violence. Drug dealers trying to push their product to adolescents may not take kindly to what they may see as self-righteous students confronting and defying them, and they may react physically against those students. Also, if an unwanted sexual situation, particularly with an older and larger partner, begins to border on rape, an attempt to leave can unexpectedly turn violent. In all situations that threaten violence, students attempting to protect themselves should examine their options very closely before acting. In circumstances such as these, the best and safest solution may be for adolescents to remain in the risk situation and protect themselves from within as much as possible. Such cases call for students to fall back to Skill Number 8, Protecting Myself in a Risk Situation, if leaving could bring more risk than staying. Remaining in a risk situation out of fear, however, does not give students an excuse to accept the risk situation and actively take part in it. Not being able to walk away from the drug dealer in no way provides adolescents with a reason to inject drugs. If they have successfully completed an effective AIDS education program, they should be equipped with practical skills to avoid as much of the risk as possible.

10 **Dealing with Rejection.** Some of the actions prescribed in Skill Number 9 might be seen as extreme by members of a student's peer group and will more than likely have repercussions after they have been employed. Doing what a student knows is right can have costs in terms of disrupted friendships, loss of acceptance, rejection, and alienation from some segments of the peer group. Students should be aware of these risks before they utilize their skills to protect themselves or to leave a risk situation. If teens do not realize the possible costs that such actions might incur, they may feel betrayed when they use these skills only to find themselves rejected by their friends and peers.

Teens can survive rejection from their peers as long as they remain aware of their own identity. They may need to return to the very beginning of these skills, Talking to Myself, to remind themselves of their own desires and character. Along with self-statements such as "I know I can protect myself," adolescents may find it helpful to add, "I want to protect myself." If students face rejection, ostracism, or, sometimes even worse, teasing and taunting for having protected themselves from risk, they must turn inward to their own strength of conviction. Peer pressure can come in many different forms, but it can always be combated by a calm, level head. Instead of panicking and trying to fit in with the crowd again, students should take a moment to understand why they face the rejection they do. Is it the result of an unpopular stand they have taken? Is there a particular issue that remains unresolved? In the face of being left out, many teenagers immediately jump to negative assumptions about themselves. "They don't like me because I'm stupid"; "They don't include me because I'm ugly"; or "I'm not popular because I'm just not as cool as everybody else" are common feelings during adolescence, and it is the rare individual who does not experience them. More often than not, however, such assumptions are completely irrelevant to the issue at hand.

A situation involving students suddenly being rejected by friends who have included them up until now is likely the result of a single action, perhaps an action taken by students to protect themselves from risk. If a female does not go as far sexually as her partner wants, she does risk his rejection. If some students refrain from drinking or using the drugs in which the rest of their friends indulge, they may not be invited to any more parties. These are specific reasons for being left out. If students can recognize and identify the reasons for their being rejected, they can address them. Students can try to talk to their friends, explain their reasons for using these skills to protect themselves, and negotiate a reconciliation. If an entire group of friends shuns one student for his or her practice of self-protection, that student should try to talk to the one or two closest friends in the group to initiate reconciliation. This kind of discussion about feelings, beliefs, and values can help friends accept each other on their own terms.

Unfortunately, not all friendships can be rescued through reason and common sense. There are times when, by standing up to protect themselves and others in risk situations, students will lose friends. The complicated nature of relationships does not always include everyone looking out for each other's best interests. Some students may feel the cost of losing friends involved in risk activities is a high one, but that cost is always preferable to what students risk by putting themselves at risk. Students should both talk to themselves and listen to themselves to clarify their values and to remind themselves why they might be better off without friends unconcerned by risky behavior. It might seem like an empty platitude to an adolescent mourning a lost friendship, but friends who are willing to place themselves and others at risk are not worth having. Adolescents are in a much better position to simply start from the beginning and accumulate a new group of friends who look out for and protect each other.

Broad Application of Refusal Skills

These refusal skills have been primarily designed to protect students from situations with a risk for HIV infection. Properly taught, however, they can provide students with a sense of self-esteem and assertiveness that will be helpful in many situations throughout their lives. They can also easily be applied to other health curricula, such as sex education, and tobacco, alcohol, and drug abuse programs. These refusal skills can further be used by churches and community groups to provide a program for values and moral education. "Doing the right thing" need not apply only to protecting oneself from situations that carry the risk of HIV infection. The problem of recognizing and following through on wise and appropriate behaviors is one faced by people of any age.

7

Modeling the Skills

The skills enumerated in the previous chapter are vital to help-ing students protect themselves from the dangers of AIDS contracted through high-risk sex or drug use. However, as we have seen, sim-ply listing the skills or posting them on the classroom bulletin board will accomplish very little toward convincing students to embrace these skills and incorporate them into their lives. Students must in-stead be trained in how to employ these skills so that using them be-comes second nature. Teachers and students must demonstrate the correct use of these skills for each other in realistic scenes based on anecdotes or even created from whole cloth. After proper use of the skills has been demonstrated, or modeled, for them, all students must be provided with the opportunity to rigorously practice imple-menting the skills through monitored role-play assignments. This chapter will provide teachers with structured methods and plot lines for effective modeling. Role-playing and other teaching strategies will be discussed in the next chapter.

Although many of the skills seem quite simple and commonsensible, they can be more difficult to apply to real-life situations than they appear. High-risk situations that call for these skills are often quite emotional and do not always allow for clear thinking by participants. When teachers, assistants, or other students model the skills before a classroom full of students, they provide examples of how the students can use the skills in their own lives.

After the skills have been introduced and thoroughly discussed, teachers can themselves model correct behavior that incorporates the skills, or they can ask an assistant or peer educator to do so. Seeing the skills in action will be an important step for students to understand how to incorporate them into their own lives. Students learn by example, and the modeling of these refusal skills is one of the most obvious and effective methods of providing that example to them.

Modeling risk-reduction behavior for students essentially boils down to performing skits to illustrate that behavior. This is similar to the role-playing activities that the students themselves will be called upon to do later, but it does not include the same level of improvisation and ad-libbing. The more basic skills require only one person, while the advanced skills need two, whom we will call the Tempter and the Temptee. When two people take part, a rough plot line can be devised ahead of time, so that both participants know what to expect. If possible, teachers can plan a scenario with another teacher or an aide. If no other adult participants are feasible, the teacher can model the skill with a peer educator.

Each of the ten skills should be modeled individually. Although the skills build on one another, joining together to provide a full arsenal of risk-reduction behavior, they also function like a chain, with the weakest link allowing the entire structure to break down. Starting with the first skills, teachers will be able to develop a solid foundation from which to build outward, adding more complicated skills as students become prepared to execute them. Because the most important result of modeling should be student identification, teachers might want to make the situation in their first example of modeling for each skill reflect student concerns: dating, peer pressure, or other situations that teachers might identify. To avoid the assumption, which some students might be prone to make, that these skills are only aimed at them and have no relevance in the "real world," teachers might also devise a second modeling scenario that reflects their own adult concerns. Single teachers might be able to gain student identification by modeling their own worries about encountering HIV and AIDS in the dating arena and the skills they must themselves use to avoid it. Other teachers who do not have any immediate worries about confronting HIV in their personal lives might depict other situations in which they are challenged by a dilemma that tempts them to do what they should not or would rather not do. If teachers are uncomfortable revealing too much of their personal lives to their classes, these situations could easily be hypothetical.

Skill Number 1

The first few skills, as the most simple, will be the easiest for teachers to model. In preparing to model the first skill, Talking to Myself, teachers should imagine a situation in which teenagers might be tempted to do something they feel they should not do. This could be as simple as wanting to attend a party that could get out of control. For example, teachers could establish a scenario in which Charlene's parents are out of town, and Charlene is having all her friends over. This situation happened once before, and some of Charlene's friends brought beer. The teacher, modeling a teen's behavior, would practice Talking to Myself to determine whether or not to attend the party. "I got into big trouble the last time I went to Charlene's party. It won't be worth the effort to go to her house if that happens again."

To demonstrate that these skills do not have specific answers attached, that the correct response does not always have to be no, the teacher might make the scenario a little bit more complicated. "Charlene is a good friend, and I always have fun at her house, but her last party was ruined by a couple of jerks who brought beer. I want to go to the party, but I don't want to be involved with that again. I'm not sure how I'll handle it, but I know that I have the ability to stay out of trouble." This scenario demonstrates the ability of skill-users to compromise. Skill-users are not kept from doing anything fun at all, they just try to avoid trouble.

All this dialogue that the teacher is modeling would, of course, usually occur internally. Speaking it aloud is just an example to the students. Still, making oral statements sometimes provides those statements with an extra power. When students are at home, they might talk to themselves out loud in front of a mirror. Speaking them aloud gives these statements a sense of authority and can leave the speakers with a stronger determination to follow through with their decisions. Even when they are in public, students might be encouraged to whisper the statements under their breath or mumble them to themselves if it gives them strength.

Talking to Myself is the foundation for all the skills that follow, and each skill will incorporate some aspects of it. Because it seems like a small jump to other skills, such as Setting Limits, Recognizing a Risk Situation, or Making a Decision, some teachers might be tempted to add those other skills to the discussion at this time. Students, however, will benefit from as much isolation between skills as possible. If the skills start to merge one into another in the classroom, students who attempt to incorporate them into their lives are likely to skip over important parts of each skill.

An example of a situation that the teacher might find personally relevant, and that would prove that the skills are universal, might be a teacher, overworked already, who is approached by the principal to accept sponsorship of the school camera club. This hypothetical teacher is a photography buff who would love to sponsor the camera club, but he or she already sponsors two clubs and coaches the track team during the spring. The teacher's inclination might be to accept the extra assignment, thus indulging a personal interest and making the principal happy. Accepting that assignment, however, would mean becoming overextended—if the camera club itself did not suffer from a lack of attention, one or more of the teacher's other assignments would. In modeling Talking to Myself, the teacher might say just that: "I like photography, and I'd love to work with the camera club, but I just don't have enough time. For my own sake, as well as the camera club's, I'll have to turn down the assignment. I want to do what the principal asks of me, but if I just can't do it, the results will be even worse than saying no to my principal."

Skill Number 2

Listening to Myself requires a model that is very similar to Skill Number 1. Listening to Myself is in many ways the flip side of Talking to Myself, and often goes hand in hand with that skill. Still, it is important to separate them as much as possible for the purposes of modeling. The more students are able to differentiate between the skills, the more they will be sure they are using them correctly.

We will continue to use the same scenario of Charlene's party to model this skill. It is not always necessary to carry the same scenarios or characters through all the skills modeling. In fact, because this process is likely to occur over a period of a few days, it may even become unwieldy, as some students will forget the particulars of the characters and situations. For our purposes, however, carrying the same situation through a number of skills can demonstrate how the skills fit together and build upon one another.

After Talking to Myself and remembering the troubles caused by Charlene's last party, the teacher modeling the skill can explore any feelings associated with that experience:

> Last time, Mom and Dad got very angry at me. They grounded me for a week. How did that make me feel? I remember feeling angry at Charlene that she let anybody bring beer in the first place. I was also angry with my parents for punishing me, but I felt like I'd let them down, too. I felt a little bit ashamed, because I know better than to put myself in that situation. So what do I feel now, when the situation is coming up again? Well, I'm a little bit scared, because I don't want the same thing to happen a second time. I have a nervous feeling in my stomach, and that tells me that I think it might happen again. But Charlene got in trouble over that last party, too, and she might know better this time. I do feel confidence in Charlene, and I really think she might've learned her lesson. Still, I'm not completely sure. But I don't want to miss a good party. Everybody else will probably be there, and I expect that I'll have a good time, as long as it doesn't get out of control again.

Teachers should explain to students that identifying and clarifying their feelings will help them understand just what decision they want to make when they reach the Making a Decision skill. Understanding these feelings makes it much easier to act on them. In the scenario above, the character has conflicting emotions about attending the party. We often have mixed feelings about situations, and modeling such for students just affirms that these feelings are natural. Students should not be led to believe that their feelings about controversial situations will be clear cut. If this were the case, they would never need to implement Listening to Myself, because it would be obvious to them what they were feeling.

Teachers showing the relevance of the skills to their own experience can also build on the professional scenario outlined above. After being approached by the principal to sponsor the camera club, they can ask themselves the same question they suggest to students:

"How do I feel?" An answer might be:

> I feel flattered that the principal has enough confidence in me to
> add another responsibility to my job. I'd also love to sponsor the
> camera club. I haven't had enough time lately to take pictures like
> I used to, and this gives me the perfect excuse. On the other hand,
> the whole thing makes me a bit anxious. The reason I haven't been
> taking pictures lately is because I've had so much to do at school.
> Even though I've already noticed that I'm flattered by the princi-
> pal's confidence, I'm also annoyed that she would just pile some-
> thing more on top of me when she already knows I have too much
> to do. No one wants to say no to their boss, but I feel that she might
> just be taking advantage of my good nature.

Skill Number 3

Setting Limits is not a skill that should be limited to particular situations. This skill must act as a preassigned barrier. To employ this
skill most effectively, students should set aside a time to sit down and
consider risks that they are likely to encounter. It may seem silly to
them to make an effort to think about what they would do if a friend
offered them a beer, or if a romantic interest wanted to go to bed
with them, but the better prepared they are when they actually confront such a situation, the more effectively they will be able to deal
with it.

An effective scenario for Setting Limits will not be as lively as the
party scenario that we have been discussing so far and to which we
will soon return. The best scenario for the teacher to model is that
described above: to simply sit down and consider what risks a student might face and to decide how to stay away from those risks.
The final purpose of AIDS prevention education is, obviously, to prevent HIV infection, so that would be an obvious risk to use in modeling Skill Number 3. The teacher can sit at the front of the classroom, pretend to be in a bedroom, living room, or other comfortable
place, and say aloud, "I don't want to become infected with HIV.
What should I do to avoid it?" Talking to Myself and Listening to
Myself become very important components of the process of Setting
Limits. Students should be reminded to actually implement these
skills at this time. Thinking about limits and vaguely reaching a conclusion will not be good enough. Instead, students must use the
skills they have learned so far to make concrete decisions about their
limits.

Teachers modeling this skill should specify precise behaviors that put students at risk for HIV infection, such as drinking or using drugs before a sexual situation, which might lead to a lowered resistance to refusing sexual intercourse. "I have learned to identify risky behaviors," the teacher might begin, "and I can set limits in my life to help me avoid those behaviors. I know that drinking or taking drugs can make me think less clearly. In that kind of situation, I might make a mistake that I could come to regret later." Skill Number 1 is already a part of Setting Limits, and Skill Number 2 can be brought into use as well:

> How do I feel about my risk of becoming infected with HIV? To be honest, I really don't feel that I am at risk. I understand that anybody is potentially at risk, but my friends aren't really those kinds of people. However, I need to remember that no one ever thinks they are at risk for HIV infection. Instead of just assuming that I should be safe, I need to think realistically about the risk. I know I can't tell who might be infected by looking at them, so there is really no way I can know who presents a risk of infection and who doesn't. Because of that, I need to make sure that I never put myself into a position where any risk could possibly be present. I know that I would not be as careful in taking care of myself if I take drugs or have too many drinks. Now that I am sober and clear-headed, I must decide how much I can drink before it affects me too much.

Teachers should remember to keep any suggested limits within realistic bounds. Some students might comfortably choose to abstain from all illicit substances and set that as a limit. Others, however, will not want to accept what they see as a drastic limit. Insisting that they do so may well cause such students to dismiss most or all of these refusal skills altogether. Rather than jeopardizing the entire process, teachers should remain open to alternate limits.

In modeling this skill, teachers should see the creation of limits through to the particulars. "How does drinking affect me? I find that after I have one beer, I start feeling self-conscious, and after two, I just don't make any sense to myself. I don't trust myself to avoid trouble after two beers, so I'd be better off to stop after one." The limit of one beer, then, would be set and would be presented by the teacher as immutable for the hypothetical student he or she is modeling.

The adult scenario would function in much the same way. The teacher would examine what kind of work commitments he or she was willing to make:

> I'm already stretched with the track team and the two clubs I sponsor, and any more work would make those groups or my teaching itself suffer. To keep my sanity, I can only allow myself to do so much. I have to stop with one team and two clubs. Three clubs would just leave me too overwhelmed.

Skill Number 4

Many adults may mistakenly think that Recognizing a Risk Situation would be a very easy skill to demonstrate and convey. In making this assumption, however, they have likely forgotten their own teen years. By the time they reach adulthood, people have accumulated a certain amount of experience to help them spot trouble. Teenagers, however, are still in the process of accumulating that experience and cannot always recognize and avoid trouble so easily.

Teachers are advised to return to the previous scenario of Charlene's party to model Skill Number 4. When students are beginning to learn this skill, they are likely to have very weak instincts to differentiate high-risk situations from less risky ones. Therefore, they should examine every potential situation they are entering for possible risk. When considering Charlene's party, the hypothetical student should very consciously ask the question, "Will there be any risky situations there?" The answer can follow quickly: "There could be, because there was one last time. If Charlene invites the same people, they might very well bring beer with them again. I'll need to review my limit and make a decision about the party based on that."

Charlene's party is a very easy risk situation to recognize because of the history involved. Teachers may want to model a situation that does not have an obvious precedent. Many people go out together after school sporting events, and the teacher can present a situation in which a teen is invited to go out with John and Chuck to get a pizza after a basketball game. Teachers should reflect on this invitation by asking pointed questions. "How well do I know John and Chuck? Have I heard anything suspicious about them?" Even if the hypothetical student does not have a precedent of going out for pizza to fall back on, he or she should know if John and Chuck have a reputation for getting into trouble. "I've known Chuck most of my life, and somehow, even though he seems to mean well, things just seem to go wrong when we're together. This might not be such a good idea." To prove that every situation is not a risky one, however, the student can decide in John and Chuck's favor. "John, Chuck, and I always have a good time together, and we've never had any problems in school. Every Monday, they come in and tell stories about the fun they've had on the weekend, and I'm glad that I'll finally be able to join them."

The John and Chuck scenario might have very different consequences depending on whether the hypothetical student modeled by the teacher is male or female. A male student would only have the question of joining John and Chuck to pal around, but a female might see another agenda:

> John's had a crush on me all year, and he's tried to go out with me before. I like him as a friend, but I don't want to get involved with him. If I went to the pizza parlor with him and Chuck, he might think that I'm more interested than I really am. That could put me in an uncomfortable position.

Teachers using the camera club scenario might find Skill Number 4 more difficult to model, because the offer of this club is an obvious risk situation. Two clubs was the preset limit, and the third club blatantly surpasses it. Still, going through the inner dialogue can provide a good example for students. Some risk situations they will encounter will be rather blatant. It can be good to reinforce the expectation that not every potential circumstance is ambiguous. Students may be reassured to realize that, upon occasion, they will easily be able to recognize the risk inherent in a situation.

Skill Number 5

Making a Decision is the meeting point of the two previous skills, where a risk situation and a student's preset limits intersect. On the surface, Skill Number 5 appears to offer students several possible reactions. If students have properly laid the groundwork from the previous skills, however, their options in Making a Decision are actually quite limited. In the case of Charlene's party, the risk situation is the possible presence of beer and the preset limit is drinking one beer. The obvious decision that a student would make, then, is to attend the party and drink no more than one beer. The teacher modeling this skill can simply put those pieces together like a puzzle.

Some discretion can come into play, however, if a particular risk situation suggests a more stringent limit. In this case, the student would be wise to review his or her limits:

> I have decided to have no more than one beer, because two or more throws my judgment off. The last time Charlene had a party, however, I got into trouble just because beer was present at all. Maybe in this case, I should add a tighter limit. After Listening to Myself and my reactions to the possibility of getting into trouble again, I'm going to decide to go to the party but to leave quickly if any beer or wine shows up. That will prove to my parents that I'm responsible and interested in staying clear of problems.

Even though the student has decided that he or she can drink one beer without running the risk of clouding judgment, this particular situation calls for avoiding beer altogether.

Just as with Skill Number 4, teachers modeling the adult scenario will find Making a Decision relatively easy to demonstrate. Because the teacher set a limit of two clubs and one sport, the principal's offer of a third club must be turned down. To show that some consideration is necessary, however, the teacher can consider differing ways of handling the problem. The teacher's preset limit was two clubs, so another club is not an acceptable alternative, but if the camera club is a tempting enough proposition, the teacher might suggest a trade to the principal. In order to take on sponsorship of the camera club, the teacher might offer to hand the sponsorship of another club to someone else. Therefore, instead of a simple yes or no answer, the teacher can put forward a compromise. This will demonstrate to students that decision-making does not have to remain black and white.

Skill Number 6

After a number of skills involving internal processes, Giving No for an Answer finally moves the refusal skills toward taking external action. Continuing with the scenario of Charlene's party, we have finally reached the point where our hypothetical skill-user is attending the party, and someone has brought a twelve-pack of beer. Once the student is aware of the beer, he or she must fall back to Skill

Number 1 and Skill Number 2, Talking to Myself and Listening to Myself, to get his or her bearings in the situation.

> I didn't want this to happen, and I'm more than a little annoyed that Charlene couldn't keep the beer out. How do I feel about this now that it's happened? First, I wish it hadn't, because I've been having a good time. I'm disappointed that I have to act on this decision now. But now that alcohol is here, I feel very uneasy. I got in trouble before, and I'm afraid I can get in trouble again. I want to leave, but I'm worried that everyone else will think I'm a baby for leaving. So it looks like any decision I reach will make me uncomfortable for a little while. I guess I'll just have to decide what is better in the long run. I don't want to get in trouble at home again, so I should pay attention to the decision I made before I came. I can just tell Charlene that I'm leaving because I'm tired so I won't feel embarrassed.

This scenario again illustrates that risk situations are often ambiguous. While there will usually be a "best" option, more often than not, that option will carry some negative aspects itself. After Talking to Myself, students will be in a good position to understand their feelings as they review the limits they had previously set as part of Skill Number 3.

To make the situation even more true to life, the teacher modeling this skill might physically take a step or two, stop, and reconsider. "Maybe I won't get in trouble this time. I can probably stay and have a good time." After saying this, the teacher should stop, perhaps even by physically putting up his or her hands to demonstrate the stopping and saying "Stop." The teacher should then continue: "I promised myself that I would stay out of trouble and leave this party if I saw any beer. I've seen beer now, so I'm going to keep my promise to myself and leave." At this point, the teacher should resolutely walk away.

The adaptability of the skills can be demonstrated in the scenario of the teacher Giving No for an Answer to the principal. As with the teenage scenario, the teacher presenting this scenario to the class should recruit a helper to play the part of the principal. After summarizing the thought process of the previous five skills that has helped the hypothetical teacher reach this point, the teacher can turn down the principal's offer. Again, making sure that true-to-life problems are represented, the principal should make turning down the offer as difficult as possible. "We don't have anyone to take over the camera club," the principal might respond. "If you won't take it, we'll have to disband the club altogether." The teacher should stand his or her ground, retorting:

> If I take on that added responsibility my other obligations will suffer. It wouldn't be fair to the track team or to the other clubs I sponsor. Instead of just the camera club being harmed, all of my responsibilities will also suffer. There's also the possibility that my classes would start to show the strain. You'll just have to find someone else.

To demonstrate that such confrontations are no easier for adults than they are for teenagers, the teacher might step out of the scenario from time to time to illustrate the usefulness of previous skills, most particularly Talking to Myself. "I won't let the principal talk me into taking this on. I know it would be a mistake. I can say no and mean it. I'm not going to walk away from this conversation with an extra responsibility." To portray the seriousness of the situation, the teacher might fall back on a technique suggested above, putting his or her hands up as if to ward off a perceived attack, saying, "No, no, no!" This would represent an interior monologue of which the principal would be unaware, but the power of revealing it to the class is undeniable. If they realize that even teachers and other adults must rely upon such measures to effectively stave off risky situations, students will be much more likely to adopt the skills themselves.

Skill Number 7

After students go public with the decision they have made, they should be prepared to experience opposition. No one wants to be thought of as a killjoy, always prepared to put an end to everyone else's fun, and peer pressure is often the strongest single barrier to Making a Decision and Giving No for an Answer. Teens will be afraid that if they walk away from their friends in too many risk situations, their friends will stop inviting them to participate in anything. Throughout our lives, our reputations are among our most important attributes, and if students gain a reputation of being no fun, or worse, of ruining other people's fun, they will have a difficult time making and holding on to friends. Students who believe that losing their friends will be the fate assigned to them if they utilize these refusal skills will ignore everything the teacher is trying to accomplish. Skill Number 7, Offering Alternatives, is intended to keep this awful destiny at bay. It allows students to continue the conversation after establishing that their answer is no.

Returning to our scenario of Charlene's party, we can see how Skill Number 7 can easily be added. Our hypothetical skill-user, having set a limit of leaving the party if alcohol becomes apparent and having been confronted with the presence of alcohol, has decided to leave. In Skill Number 6, we saw this person make the decision to tell Charlene about this decision and leave the party. Now, Skill Number 7 broadens the list of options available to the teen. Instead of walking away from the party, our protagonist can make some other suggestions. Earlier in the evening, perhaps at the same time he or she was coming to the decision to leave the party at the first trace of alcohol, the student might have been developing backup plans. While the student was using Talking to Myself and Listening to Myself to determine the possible risk that might arise at the party and Setting Limits to decide upon a response, he or she might also have used the time to consider alternative activities. If the skill-user has come up with two alternatives, for instance, then he or she can have them at the ready when the time comes to act. Thus, the skill-user does not have to face the fear of an unknown situation but, rather, can relax and offer alternative number one and, if that is not accepted, alternative number two.

One alternative that the student may have devised might be to give Charlene the choice—"Get rid of the alcohol or I'm leaving." If the student had been concerned about the possibility of alcohol soon enough, he or she might have already had a conversation with Charlene to identify this concern. "We all got in trouble last time," the student might say, "so make sure nobody's going to bring beer." Charlene's response to this advice would likely have had some bearing on the student's decision to go to the party in the first place. If Charlene said, "I can't help it if some of my guests want to bring beer, and I'm not going to stop them," the student might have had second thoughts about attending. If, on the other hand, Charlene said, "You know, you're right, and I'm going to tell people that I don't want them to bring anything," the student would have attended the party with more confidence. Given the first option, that the student and Charlene had discussed the situation earlier, a confrontation with Charlene at the party is a possibility. If that discussion did not take place, however, forcing Charlene to take care of the alcohol problem is not terribly realistic.

A second alternative to the student simply leaving the party and going home might be for the teen to gain the support of another group of friends attending Charlene's party. Although they may feel like it, teens in this sort of predicament are often not alone. Although peer pressure might make it appear that everyone else at the party wants to indulge in and enjoy the alcohol that has appeared, a number of people would rather that the challenge had never been set in front of them. Teens feeling at risk in the situation can find like-minded allies. Our skill-user might look around to identify such people and make alternative plans with them. If a number of people want to leave Charlene's party because of the risk that they see developing, the skill-user may find safety, and fun, in numbers.

To continue following our example of how Offering Alternatives can be employed in the adult scenario, the teacher can back up from the position in which he or she was left at the end of Skill Number 6, categorically refusing to take on the added responsibility of the camera club. There are few other possibilities open to the teacher. He or she cannot, for example, cut back on working hours. One area that can be affected, however, might be the teacher's other responsibilities—the two other clubs and the track team. As we saw earlier, the teacher would have the option of suggesting that one of these obligations be passed along to someone else. "I can't take on more than two clubs at one time," the teacher might say, "but I'd be happy to let someone else take up the slack by sponsoring either the science club or the FFA." With this response, the teacher proves that he or she is not refusing any change at all but is willing to work with the principal. After the teacher offers alternatives, the principal may realize that some compromise can be reached. The conversation about the camera club will continue, rather than be cut short. The teacher is thus able to hold on to a reputation of being helpful and cooperative rather than obstructionist.

Skill Number 8

Although the primary purpose of Protecting Myself in a Risk Situation is to promote the avoidance of unsafe sex, it can be helpful in nonsexual risk situations as well. When teens are faced with a situation in which they have already given no for an answer, and the alternatives they have offered have not been accepted, they are left with only two options: leaving the situation, or staying and protecting themselves. Leaving a Risk Situation will be dealt with in Skill Number 9, allowing us to focus here on staying.

This skill, perhaps more than any other, falls back on the first two skills, Talking to Myself and Listening to Myself. Instead of spurring people to action, Skill Number 8 in many cases motivates its users to do nothing. Therefore, students employing this skill must constantly talk to themselves, reminding themselves of their limits and encouraging themselves to reject any temptation to exceed those limits. The goal of Protecting Myself in a Risk Situation is no more than to maintain an equilibrium, to keep the status quo.

Even though Skill Number 8's goal is simple and straightforward, it must not be modeled in a simplistic way. Protecting oneself is more complicated than just saying no. The difficulty of resisting temptation and peer pressure must play a part in any modeling that the teacher presents. Charlene's party provides an excellent example of this. Alcohol has become available at the party, and our hypothetical student has previously set a limit of leaving if and when this occurred. If the student had his or her own car, this would not be a problem, but there are any number of reasons why the student might not have a car available. Perhaps the student came with someone else who does not want to leave. Perhaps the student made arrangements with his or her parents to be picked up at a particular time. If the parents had their own plans for the evening, they might not be available to come back early. For whatever reason the teacher chooses to use, the student is not able to leave the party and maintain his or her stated limit. What happens next? Since the limit has been overstepped, should the student throw caution to the winds and partake in the beer? After all, as we saw in the discussion of Skill Number 5, this student does extend the limit to one beer from time to time. Maybe, since leaving is not an option, the teen should just sit back, have a beer, and enjoy the party. Such an option, however, is obviously not a good idea. The idea of establishing a limit before entering into a situation is to determine what might be safe behavior and what is not. The behavior that was identified as risky before the party remains risky whether the student can carry out the preset limit or not. Teens should stay as close as possible to the spirit of their limits whenever they cannot follow the letter.

In order to successfully resist temptation, the teacher modeling this skill must make sure that worthy temptations are offered. Two or three other people should be recruited to help model this skill, offering a beer to the skill-user, applying peer pressure to get the student to take a drink, and perhaps even taunting and making fun of the student for refusing. During this process, the teacher can model the inner dialogue that would likely be taking place. When confronted by a friend offering beer, the teacher will fall back on Talking to Myself to remind the class of the original limit. "I already decided that I wasn't going to have anything to drink tonight, and I'm not going to go back on my promise to myself. If I did, I'd just feel guilty and awful later. I'd be furious with myself tomorrow morning." In refusing the beer, the teacher modeling the skill does not need to make a self-righteous stand of any sort, explaining why he or she is refusing to have a drink. A polite refusal can often more than serve the purpose. "No thanks, you go ahead and have it. I just don't feel like a beer tonight." If this student can simply shrug off the advance, other people attending the party are less likely to press the issue. However, in order to demonstrate this skill in action, the teacher should raise the stakes and arrange for one or two more assistants to ridicule the student for not taking a drink. They might call the student "chicken," or any other epithets the teacher is comfortable using in the classroom. No one likes to be on the receiving end of this kind of behavior, and most if not all students in the class will relate to the skill-user the teacher is modeling. The teacher's goal in this situation, then, is to remain cool and level headed. To demonstrate this process, the teacher should model any positive thoughts aloud. "I can enjoy this party without having any beer. I can make my own decisions. I don't have to knuckle under to the influence of others." This model scenario will show that using these skills is not always easy, and that they take some effort. When students are told honestly about this endeavor, they will be more likely to treat it with the seriousness it deserves.

When this skill is applied in sexual situations, it will usually involve some measure of negotiation. The most obvious scenario, of course, would be in the question of condom use. Teachers are urged to model such a scenario if it is at all possible in their school system. Teen lives can more easily be ruined by the consequences of unprotected sex than by virtually anything else average teens are likely to do. The scenario to be modeled would involve only two people. The two teens in the modeled scenario would be approaching sexual intercourse, but only one wants to use a condom. In a stereotypical scenario, the teen resisting the condom would likely be the male, but this will not be true in every situation. Teachers can alternate the resistance from one gender to another in different classes. The most probable point of negotiation would be "no sex without a condom," but the skill-user would not need to be confrontational about the issue. Firmly stating his or her opinion is enough. "I'm concerned that if we practice unsafe sex we can expose each other to AIDS, VD, or pregnancy. A condom can avoid all that," the teen might say. His or her partner can respond with what have become clichés in such a position. "I'm clean. I don't have any diseases. If you really loved me, you'd trust me." The trust argument can be very powerful, and teachers would do well not to disregard it. The modeled teen should respond steadfastly that trust is not a question. "I do trust you, and I don't think you'd ever want to give me a disease if you knew that you had one," the skill-user should reply. "But," he or she should continue, "you might have an infection and not even know it. I'd never give anything to you, either, but I could have an infection without knowing it, and I could pass it on to you. Besides, even if neither of us is infected, trust never stopped a woman from getting pregnant." The other teen should put up some more protests, but the skill-user must not sway. Bold teachers might include methods of making the condom more appealing, such as suggesting that the female partner put the condom on the male. If the couple can make the use of a condom more erotic and exciting, the barriers to its use will become weaker. The scenario can end in an agreement to use a condom and follow through with the intercourse, or in no intercourse if the other teen stubbornly refuses to accept a condom. The choice of no intercourse does not necessarily preclude other pleasurable activity such as mutual masturbation or other stimuli. Although many parents might prefer the choice of no activity at all, it is important that students recognize that these skills provide them with more options than just saying no. When teens are allowed to make their own decisions, they will be more likely to take what they have learned in an AIDS education program to heart.

Protecting Myself in a Risk Situation is more difficult to apply to our scenario of the teacher and principal. This skill usually goes into play when, for whatever reason, Giving No for an Answer did not bring an end to the risk situation. As this would apply to the adult scenario, the teacher would be in a position where he or she must take on the added responsibility of the camera club with no possibility of moving another club to someone else. The risk in this scenario was the danger of becoming overextended, so to gain adequate protection, the teacher would have to devise a schedule that addressed the problem. This could be modeled through a monologue in which the teacher comes to this realization. "I'll have less time to myself if I take on the camera club, but if I figure out my scheduling properly, I think I can fit it all in." Negotiation can also be added if the teacher and principal compromise that the situation will be only temporary. If this is the case, the modeled teacher can demonstrate that he or she did everything possible to protect himself or herself in this situation.

Skill Number 9

Leaving a Risk Situation is a last-ditch effort, when everything else has failed. Many risk situations will not progress this far, but students should be well acquainted with what the skill entails. In some ways, however, Skill Number 9 may be the easiest of the skills to model. This skill does not require a lot of reflection or decision-making. Rather, once all other options have been exhausted—there are no more alternatives to offer and little chance of effectively protecting oneself—leaving the situation becomes the only realistic choice. The situation has become too dangerous to risk staying, so leaving becomes a decision reached out of necessity rather than any other reasoning process.

If the decision to leave a risk situation is a mostly self-evident one, then the modeled scenario should demonstrate how the skill-user would reach this realization. The student at Charlene's party has reached the end of the line. The preset limit was to stay out of the presence of beer at the party. Beer did appear, so the student was forced to make a decision and give no for an answer. After an offered alternative that Charlene get rid of the beer so the party could remain alcohol-free is rejected, the student has no choice but to leave. The only question remaining is how the student will carry out that action. In the model for Skill Number 7, he or she has already suggested to some other friends that they leave together and go somewhere that will be alcohol-free. If the other friends have agreed, then the group can all leave together, causing very few problems. Obviously, this is a best-case scenario and will happen often enough to make it a worthwhile model. The modeled skill-user should suggest to the group of friends, "Listen, there's no point staying around here any longer, so let's just go." To demonstrate that these friends are leaving with a plan, someone might mention the place they have decided to go.

In some instances, of course, students will not be able to convince any friends to leave the party with them, and this possibility should be modeled as well. Here, the skill-user should confront some opposition to carrying out the decision to leave the party. This can be in the form of friends trying to convince the student to stay. Some of these friends might be quite innocent in their protestations: "Come on, we're having a good time. Don't leave now." Others might be more pointed, perhaps even Charlene herself: "So, you just can't stand the heat, huh? As soon as the beer comes, you have to make a beeline for the door." The teacher modeling this skill should once again give students a view into the model's thinking process, using the skill of Talking to Myself. "I've already made my decision. I've thought about my reasons for leaving, and I'm going to go through with it." The student does not need to make a detailed argument on behalf of leaving. If the student would rather just get it over with, he or she might say something like: "I was feeling kind of tired anyway, so I'm just going to go on home." He or she does not need to justify the action being taken. In fact, some students may be more comfortable saying nothing at all on their way out the door. Others may want to make some sort of polite good-bye to Charlene. The most important thing to do is to follow through on the goal. Some students might be reluctant to leave under such circumstances, worried that everyone at the party will gossip about their behavior after they are gone. Although some gossip may be raised for a few minutes after the student leaves, most people at the party will not take much notice. More often than not, the other teens at the party have their own concerns to worry about.

As suggested in the last chapter, there are some more dangerous situations that might be exacerbated by trying to leave. An attempt to leave could be met with violence. Before trying to walk out of any risk situation, students should take a moment or two to examine the type of situation they are in. If students find themselves in the midst of a drug deal, for instance, they would be far better off keeping a low profile and riding the encounter out.

Although it does not include the same element of danger, an example of a situation in which leaving is not possible would be the teacher-and-principal scenario we have been following. The only

way that the teacher could leave the situation of expanded responsibilities would be to resign from his or her position. This is hardly a
realistic option, so this scenario can serve as an illustration to students of how individuals faced with a risk situation must sometimes
choose the least of the various evils available. This would be an instance that demonstrates that these refusal skills cannot always elim-
inate a risk situation but can certainly lower the amount of risk.
Because the teacher in this scenario has followed the refusal skills,
he or she has examined the situation and uncovered his or her true
feelings surrounding the camera club. Also, by discussing the situation with the principal, the teacher has let the principal know the
problems that could arise and has laid the groundwork for a future
reexamination of the issue if the teacher does indeed become overwhelmed by the workload. Although the teacher has had to reluc-
tantly accept sponsorship of the camera club, he or she is definitely
in a better position with the principal for having used the skills.

Skill Number 10

Teachers should allow their students to have no misconceptions
about the costs that are sometimes involved in using these refusal
skills. Some of the stands that students will be encouraged to take
will be unpopular and may cost them friends. While it may be true
that students are better off without friends who would abandon
them for staying true to their principles, such a statement provides
little consolation for a teen who feels rejected by peers. Teachers
should also not attempt to downplay the rifts between friends that
may occur. There is certainly no need to dwell on these negatives
and potentially scare students away from using the skills at all, but
some recognition is advised.

We can return a final time to the scenario featuring Charlene's
party to see how this skill might be modeled. Although some peer
disapproval might be apparent during the party or as the hypothetical student is leaving, this skill is primarily intended to address any
long-term rejection that students might face. The model might begin after the student has experienced some sort of snub or rebuff.
This could be a direct statement made by a friend at school or over
the phone, an overheard comment between two friends, a party to
which the student was not invited, or even nothing more than an
intuitive recognition that various relationships with friends are not

quite right. The first thing that the student should do after this real-ization is to determine what the cause might be. People do not usu-ally drop their friends on a whim. If a rift has formed in the rela-tionship, it most likely will be because of a particular, identifiable event. In this case, it could very possibly be the stand the student took at Charlene's party. Without a partner, the teacher can model aloud the thoughts that a student in this position might be thinking. "I can tell everyone is acting differently toward me. Sometimes I think it's just because I'm a jerk, but I know that that's not true. I'm the same as I was last week, and nobody was avoiding me then. The only thing that's different is that I left Charlene's party when some of those guys brought beer. It was the right thing to do then, and I'd do the same thing again, even if everybody treats me this way. I don't think that walking out of the party is a good enough reason for them to act like this."

Essentially, students in this position have two choices. They can wait until the trouble blows over, which usually happens. Although they might deserve one, they should not expect an apology of any sort. What is most likely to happen is that friends who go out of their way to snub these students will simply get over it and begin to allow the students back into the fold. Patience can win out in a situ-ation like this, but unfortunately, patience is not always a strong suit of teenagers. The teacher can try to model an internal dialogue along these lines: "I'm more stubborn than they are, and I'm going to wait until they come to their senses. I refuse to let their rejection get to me."

If students prefer to be more active in seeking the approval of their peers, they might approach one or two of their closest friends among those shunning them for some sort of reconciliation. The teacher can model the teen explaining why he or she did what he or she did and telling these friends that using the refusal skills should never be taken as the skill-user's rejection of them. Students' first responsibility in protecting themselves must be to themselves, not to anyone else. Many teens will accept this type of heart-to-heart dis-cussion and will take the first step in bringing the skill-user back into the good graces of the peer group. It must be stressed to the stu-dents, however, that they stand their ground for using the refusal skills. They should never seek readmission to the peer group at the cost of themselves, their principles, or their self-respect. If they feel that acceptance is more important than anything else, they must remind themselves that they did the right thing. They must only seek acceptance on their own terms, not on someone else's.

The teacher can also apply Skill Number 10 to close out the camera club scenario as well. After turning down the sponsorship of this club, the teacher could very well feel some sort of aloofness on the part of the principal. In the worst case, this could result in poorer performance evaluations and fewer job perks and opportunities. It is a sad fact, unfortunately, that adults often carry grudges longer than teenagers, and the teacher cannot assume that the friction will blow over. Some sort of action will likely be necessary to return the relationship to the way it was. The teacher can model an approach to the principal to iron things out. The principal will have his or her own pressures, and a sponsorship of the camera club might be high among them. If someone else has been brought in to sponsor the club, then the principal may feel only that the teacher is uncooperative. In this case, the teacher can again outline his or her position to the principal of why sponsoring the club was not an option and offer to cooperate in other ways. Such a move would almost be like falling back on Skill Number 7, Offering Alternatives. These suggestions should be comprised of demands that might stretch the teacher but would be possible. Possibilities might be to offer to work the basketball concession stand once or twice more a week than previously scheduled or to replace the principal in monitoring a study hall so that the principal is freed up to attend to his or her other responsibilities. Such proposals would prove the teacher's willingness to cooperate and work with the principal to achieve a smoother-running workplace.

If the principal was able to find no sponsor for the camera club and has either had to take it on alone or disband the organization, he or she would likely feel that the teacher has personally let the principal down. This would be a more difficult situation for the teacher to overcome. No matter what the teacher might try to do, the principal is likely to remain unresponsive. The teacher must recognize that the situation cannot be improved and must come to grips with that fact. In front of the class, the AIDS education instructor could model this teacher's inner dialogue:

> I couldn't have handled even more responsibilities. There's no way
> I would have done even a passingly good job of everything. I was

right to turn down the principal. Unfortunately, the principal is likely to think less of me because of this. I know that I am doing my best, and that has to be good enough for me. I have to do my job so that I am pleased with it. I can't control how someone else reacts, whether that might be the principal or another teacher. As long as I am doing my best, that must be enough.

MODIFYING MODELING FOR YOUR CLASSROOM

In order to keep themselves interested, teachers should mix up their models as much as possible. As they become more comfortable with the entire process, teachers might ask their students to suggest scenarios. This helps ensure that the scenarios will be more realistic and closer to students' life experience. A further refinement of the modeling process, again suggested to be made after the teacher is comfortable, is to allow students to suggest how the model should act, based on their own understanding of the refusal skills. This will help students conceptualize the skills and recognize how they can be modified and applied to the specifics of different situations. Some students will have good ideas for how to handle a situation, and if the teacher demonstrates a successful student suggestion, this can provide strong reinforcement for students' expectations that they can handle such situations by themselves, if and when they encounter them. On other occasions, students might make poor suggestions, and through the modeled scenario, the teacher can show how these ideas might prove less than effective. It is far better for students to try and fail with their ideas in the classroom than to be left to experiment in the midst of a risk situation. As always, students should not be judged by the teacher or by peers for a poor suggestion. If the teacher is worried that such a possibility is present, he or she can always fall back on the anonymity of written suggestions.

MODELING AN AIDS-SPECIFIC SCENARIO

The two scenarios we have used as examples so far are relatively nonprovocative. They can be used in the vast majority of classrooms with little threat of raising uncomfortable moral issues. The true purpose of AIDS education, of course, is to teach students how to protect themselves in sexual situations. Somewhere during the modeling process, many students are likely to wonder how these skills will work in interpersonal sexual situations. If at all possible, teachers should introduce more provocative scenarios, such as that suggested for Skill Number 8. Although the principles remain the same no matter what the risk situation is, people do not always think as clearly when the subject turns to sex. As an example of a sexual model teachers might use, we can begin with an obvious scenario that demonstrates the process. Teachers modeling the skills for the first time with their class might prefer to stick with the previous scenarios, but if they desire later to delve into situations in which the risk of AIDS is more clear, this scenario will provide a good demonstration.

Our scenario involves a boyfriend, the Tempter, and a girlfriend, the Temptee. This couple has been going together for quite some time and has had some measure of intimacy, but they have not yet experienced intercourse. They have discussed that subject, however, and they expect to have intercourse soon, at a moment that seems right for both of them. As the scenario begins, the boyfriend is driving the girlfriend home after a party. He may have been drinking a bit or smoking some pot, so he is not completely lucid. As the couple arrives at the girl's home, they park in the driveway. The boyfriend starts to get amorous, and, although the girlfriend wants to kiss and fondle with him, she does not want to follow through all the way to intercourse at this time.

In this scenario, the girlfriend, the Temptee, must fall back upon her refusal skills. Because she and her boyfriend have discussed the possibility of having intercourse sometime in the future under mutually agreeable circumstances, we can assume that this is her limit: she does not intend to have intercourse until they each decide the time is right. Teachers can ask their students to identify what is wrong with this picture. The answer, of course, is that a limit as vague as this one cannot provide very much protection. The limit is subjective rather than objective.

No matter the drawbacks of this particular limit, however, it is the limit that the girlfriend has chosen. The front seat of her boyfriend's car while they are sitting in her driveway is apparently not the time of the girlfriend's choosing. The boyfriend, however, is in an amorous mood and begins to pressure her. Teachers can choose what form this pressure should take. If they are unsure about tackling this subject head on, they can simply have the boyfriend make suggestions to the girlfriend about their activity. To present their students with a more realistic and more dangerous situation, teachers might suggest that the boyfriend and girlfriend are already engaged in kissing and fondling. The boyfriend might move his hand to a position that makes the girlfriend uncomfortable. This would be a situation in which the skills cannot be broken down and followed one step at a time. At the moment the girlfriend realizes she is uncomfortable, she must enact three skills virtually simultaneously. She must Recognize Her Risk Situation, Make a Decision, and, if that decision is in keeping with her preset limit, Give No for an Answer.

The girlfriend's thought process at this point should be modeled to the class. It can be scripted ahead of time so that all the bugs have been worked out. Teachers can follow the script, showing their students how such a reasoning process would work. The girlfriend's interior monologue should be straightforward, and it need not vary too much from the other monologues we have discussed so far.

> I don't want to have intercourse with my boyfriend now. We both said we'd wait until we were both ready, and I'm not ready yet. I have to stop this before it's too late. Even though I don't want to make him mad, I know that I'll feel awful later. I'll be disappointed in myself, and I'll just be angry about the whole thing.

An assistant should stand by to portray the boyfriend when the girlfriend finishes her interior monologue and then must stop him from going forward.

Giving No for an Answer, the next step, also need not be different from the examples we have seen so far. The girlfriend can physically sit up, slightly pushing the boyfriend away. "We said we weren't going to do this yet. Not until we're both ready." The boyfriend might reply, "By the way you were acting, I thought you were ready. You sure seem ready to me, and I know I'm ready."

"I'm not ready. I'll let you know when I am," could be her reply. The teacher should stress that the girlfriend should try to remain calm in the situation. She might be somewhat upset with the boyfriend for forcing the issue, but anger and anxiety are not helpful emotions in this situation. If she demonstrates too much vulnerability, the boyfriend might assume that he can persuade his girlfriend to go ahead with the intercourse. The girlfriend should use physical cues to relay her strength, such as putting some amount of distance between the two of them, not allowing any sort of kissing or other sexual play while the discussion is continuing, and looking her boyfriend directly in the eye. Her demeanor, as much as her words, will convey the seriousness and sincerity of her position.

No matter what the boyfriend says, the girlfriend should remain steadfast. She might Offer Alternatives, suggesting how far the boyfriend might comfortably go. Perhaps she is willing to go no farther than kissing. She might accept his hands under her blouse, or even taking her blouse off. No sexual intercourse does not have to mean no physical contact whatsoever. Anything such as this that students might recognize as a realistic depiction of their experience will allow them to take the refusal skills more seriously as a possible aid in their dealing with others.

At the end of this scenario, the teacher can show that all the skills do not necessarily come into play in every situation. This scenario, featuring an established couple who are trying to deal with the question of when intercourse should be attempted, will most likely not require the final three skills, Protecting Myself in a Risk Situation, Leaving a Risk Situation, or Dealing with Rejection. This is not a new issue to them, and the boyfriend will probably be swayed by the girlfriend's arguments. He will not press the issue to where condoms must be negotiated, and he will not present a risk of physical harm so that the girlfriend must get away at any cost. If this is an ongoing discussion between them, he will also probably not reject his girlfriend out of hand and break up with her over the issue. Students should be prepared to utilize these skills, but they must not become so tied to the order that they try to use any skill when it is not necessary.

8

Skill-Building Classroom Activities

As every teacher knows, observing is no substitute for doing. Students gain a lot by watching teachers model the proper use of the refusal skills, but they will never be able to internalize the skills completely until they practice them themselves. For AIDS education to be most effective, every student must have the opportunity to engage the skills personally, to practice using the skills in the classroom. This chapter will examine methods teachers can use to bring their students into active contact with refusal skills and the AIDS curriculum.

ROLE-PLAYING

The most effective method of instilling the refusal skills in adolescents is role-playing. Students learn how to make proper use of the skills through practice and repetition. In order to assure that an AIDS education program is effective, every student must participate in role-plays and must be able to demonstrate, at least once, that he or she is capable of using the skills correctly to handle a risk situation.

Teachers incorporating role-plays into their curriculum can allow them to assume different forms. One possibility is that students can take a role in a scenario and perform for the entire class. At the end of the role-play, the teacher and the class can comment on the student's effectiveness and can suggest ways he or she might improve. Having every student play a role in front of the entire class can be very time-consuming, however, and teachers should come up with ways of conducting several role-play exercises at once. Students using the skills in role-plays should be observed, of course, or their potential failings might be overlooked and might become a regular part of their skill use. One possibility to make the process take up less time might be to include any available peer educators in the observation process. If the teacher or the school district has prepared any students to fill this role, now would be a good time to utilize them. Peer educators should be able to demonstrate the skills when necessary and also review and critique others' use of them. If a class could be divided up into groups, each led by one peer educator, each group could observe one of its members trying to use the refusal skills at the same time, allowing several role-plays to happen at once. The teacher could roam the classroom, overseeing all groups at once. This way, every student gets an opportunity to practice the skills, and the teacher saves valuable instructional time.

Another method that teachers might find helpful while conducting these role-plays is a video camera. Teachers who videotape their students using the skills in role-playing exercises will find the tape an excellent instructional tool. Reviewing the tape after a role-play, teachers and other students can point out errors to the student who has just completed the exercise. If students are allowed to see themselves somewhat more objectively, they can more easily recognize their own weak points in utilizing the skills. Once they recognize their weaknesses, they will be in a much stronger position to correct them.

Because these role-plays must reflect actual risk situations, some students may feel very self-conscious in playing the role in front of others. Teachers will have made a strong advance in combating such feelings if they have been able to establish the nonjudgmental atmosphere that was discussed earlier. If students feel that it is safe to try playing a role and that they will not be ridiculed for coming up short, they will be able to get much more out of the role-plays. This is not a time for students to simply go through the motions, because without honestly engaging themselves in learning and performing the skills, they put themselves at higher risk than is absolutely necessary. Students often feel somewhat more comfortable if they know that they are not being singled out for special consideration. If they know from the start that every student will participate, many students will feel less self-conscious. Teachers are cautioned, however, to be sensitive to the dynamics of the class and to help give everyone an even footing. Perhaps more self-confident, popular students can be among the first to participate, allowing shyer students to get accustomed to the idea of performing in front of others.

The role-plays themselves should be conducted in a manner very similar to the models. Students should demonstrate their thought processes as they relate to the situation as well as the actions they take. Teachers must know that students are making the right decisions for the right reasons. The skills are broad enough to allow a number of different interpretations, and they can be applied to various situations, but if they are not completely understood and absorbed by students, students might find themselves in a predicament where something that seemed to work in class will not work in real life. Students should be able to prove themselves capable of handling any and all unexpected turns a situation might take. Students should be deemed to have executed the role-play successfully if they have avoided all high-risk behavior. They may have recognized the risky situation and extricated themselves completely, or they may have compromised somewhat and accepted a low-risk alternative in place of a higher-risk one. This would primarily apply to sexual role-plays in which students agree to use condoms rather than to remain abstinent. Some students may have to make several attempts before they are able to navigate their way through a scenario successfully. Teachers should not make scenarios progressively easier for students who are having trouble, because those students will only be left less equipped to face the risk situations they will encounter in real life. The scenarios should be relatively challenging so that students have a better opportunity to internalize the refusal skills process. Risk situations will not be any easier to handle in students' personal lives than in the classroom. Students not properly equipped to face risk situations will succumb to them, making the effort of an AIDS education program useless.

The primary difference between role-playing and modeling is the level of preparation. Because teachers are showing their class how the refusal skills ideally work, they might use a fully scripted scenario. Teachers do not want to make an error in their models that would have to be corrected later. In order to make the experience reflect true life as much as possible, however, students should have no more than the bare bones of a situation available to them before they begin their role-play. In dramatic terms, this is called improvisation. Students should think on their feet, because that is certainly how they have to operate when they encounter risk situations outside the classroom. In preparing for a role-play, a teacher might select two students to be the Tempter and the Temptee. The Tempter might be given instructions to try to convince the other student to shoplift candy bars in a convenience store. The Temptee should have no more awareness of the situation than that he or she is spending the afternoon with a friend. Risk situations often arrive without warning, and this should be reflected in class as much as possible. Given the nature of role-plays, teachers cannot avoid putting students on their guard, a level of protection that many will not carry with them outside the classroom. Teachers should try to mix up different risk situations from time to time, so that students cannot figure out ahead of time what they will be going up against.

The first few times students role-play, the teacher and the class might take an active part in the process, coaching the Temptee on how to respond. This is good practice for students who are only observing, and it also lowers the pressure on the student in front of the class, who may feel in over his or her head for a time when following the skills. After everyone in the class has had a chance or two to participate, however, such instructions should become less frequent. If a student seems honestly stuck for a response, someone might intervene, but the longer students role-play, the more this should be kept to a minimum. This will once again reflect life outside the classroom, where assistance rarely comes along to help adolescents out of this kind of jam.

Teachers are encouraged to create their own scenarios for student role-plays. Peer educators can provide a good source of realistic scenarios. In fact, listening to and getting advice from peer educators and other students about the risk situations they sometimes face can provide an excellent source of scenarios. Circumstances taken from life will inevitably prove more useful to students than any predicament teachers can create by looking back on their own teenage years.

Teachers should also try to develop variety in the role-plays. Students in the same class will have encountered a broad range of social experiences. Some may have experience with IV drugs, while others may have never even tried smoking a cigarette. The diversity of sexual experience can be just as broad—some students may have had several partners, while others may barely be socializing with the opposite gender at all. Placing inexperienced students into a role-play in which they must negotiate their way to avoid a drug deal could be a grave mistake. The students would not want to be seen by classmates in such a situation, and to be randomly flung into it could cause distrust of the teacher and the material. A student such as this would fare better in a role-play reflecting a situation he or she might more likely encounter, such as turning down a friend who wants help in cheating on a test. As much as possible, role-plays should reflect a student's level of social sophistication.

Role-Play Scenarios

The following are a few scenarios that teachers can use until they devise their own to more closely reflect the concerns and experiences of their students. The characters in these role-plays have been given names and genders to make them easy to follow. Most characters are not gender specific and can be played by either males or females. Depending on which skills a teacher particularly wants students to model, that teacher might use all or only part of a scenario. The situation presented to students should include only that information the teacher feels is pertinent to the skill targeted by the role-play. If a teacher wants students to use their skills to avert the risk before the situation escalates to the level shown here, that teacher should give students only the first part of the scenario. Students role-playing an early part of a scenario may make the wrong decision and find themselves brought further into the plot line, where they must use their skills to extricate themselves from an even more difficult position. Teachers should avoid stepping in to correct a student who is moving in the wrong direction. Before the end of the scenario, the student will come to that realization and will have to make his or her way out of it. If a student succumbs to risky behavior in a role-play, he or she will have another chance, unlike real life, to get it right later.

1   Graffiti. All week the entire school has been talking about the big football game on Friday night with its crosstown rival. After school on Thursday, Jeff tells his friend Ruben that he has big plans for the two of them that night. "If everything works right," Jeff says, "we'll be the school heroes!" Jeff will not be more specific, but says he will be by to pick up Ruben from home at about eight o'clock. Ruben has always wanted his friends to look up to him, so he spends the evening anticipating their adventure. When Jeff arrives, Ruben gets into his car, and notices several cans of spray-paint. When Ruben asks about the spray-paint, Jeff says they are going to spray their high school name on their rival's building.

2   Too much physical involvement on first date. Although Tracy does not know Pete very well, she has had her eye on him for quite some time. Finally, they have made plans to meet at the mall and go to a movie together. When Tracy gets to the mall, however, Pete tells her he does not have enough money for a movie, and suggests that they go out driving instead. He knows a nice spot in the park where they can park and just talk. Tracy has her doubts about going with Pete, but she wants to get to know him better. She agrees. After Pete and Tracy find a parking spot at the park, Pete immediately starts putting the moves on her. Tracy likes Pete and wants to go out with him again, but she is not sure she knows him well enough to get this involved this quickly.

3   Cheating in school. Jaime is a good student who is proud of his high grade-point average. Everyone in school knows his reputation for studying hard and doing well. His best friend, Maggie, is also a good student, but this year she has been having trouble in the math class she and Jaime attend together. A midsemester exam is coming up soon, and Maggie is very worried about it. She asks Jaime to help her study for the exam, but she still has trouble understanding the material. Panicking that she is going to fail the exam, she asks Jaime to help her cheat.

4   Unprotected sex. Dwayne and Erica have been going out for almost six months. They are one of the most established couples in the school. They have not engaged in sexual intercourse yet, because Dwayne is uncomfortable with the idea. He knows that Erica had been with several other boys and is worried about disease. Erica has said she does not think she has any sexually transmitted diseases, but she has never actually gone to a doctor to check. Dwayne feels that Erica is starting to get impatient, and he would like to have intercourse with her. He wants to use condoms but is afraid that Erica will be insulted if he suggests it. He plans to bring up the subject tonight.

5   Buying drugs. Liz and Pam are hanging together after school. Pam seems sort of restless, but that is not unusual for her. She tells Liz that she has to go meet some people, but that Liz can come along if she wants. From boredom as much as anything, Liz tags along. Pam introduces her to some people Liz has seen before but never met. Liz is suspicious and thinks that Pam may be planning to buy some drugs. Pam talks to these people for a few minutes and then reaches into her pocket. She realizes that she does not have enough money and asks to borrow some from Liz. Everyone turns to look at Liz for her reaction.

6   Shoplifting. Andre and Diane have gone to the mall together. They are just walking around, going in and out of stores but not looking at anything special. While they are in a drug store, Andre notices Diane pick up a candy bar and slip it into her pocket. He is not sure if he gives her a disapproving look, but with an attitude of defiance, she looks at him, picks up another candy bar, puts it into his jacket pocket, and quickly leaves the store. Once she is out of the store, Diane turns around, looks at Andre, and starts eating her candy bar. Her look challenges him to join her.

7   Using drugs. Howie calls Malcolm on a Friday night and asks him to come over. Howie's parents are out for the evening, so they can sit around and listen to some CDs without anyone bothering them. Malcolm picks out a couple of CDs and hurries to Howie's house. They hang for a while and have some beer. After a few minutes, Howie goes into his room and brings something out—a syringe and other drug works. Malcolm had heard rumors that Howie was doing that, but he had never paid attention. Howie shoots up in his presence and then asks Malcolm if he would like to try it, too. Malcolm is a little bit curious, but he realizes that Howie has only one syringe.

8   Getting an AIDS test. Yuki has just completed an AIDS education program at his school. He has learned how HIV can be transmitted and realizes that he has behaved in ways that might have put him at risk. He does not know anyone who is HIV-positive, though, so he thinks he is probably safe. His teacher had told the class that anyone who has had a history of risky behavior should get an AIDS test, but Yuki is sure that he does not have HIV. Maybe he just should not worry about it.

9   Skipping school. Kevin borrowed his mother's car to drive to school today. He tells Pilar that he does not feel like going to his afternoon classes and suggests that they skip school together. Pilar always has fun with Kevin and knows that they would have a good time, but she is not sure that she really wants to cut school. During lunch, Kevin tries to talk Pilar into the idea. He makes a good argument and is close to convincing her to go with him.

10 Buying condoms. Keiko and Randy have been going out for about a month. Their relationship is good, and each time they are together they go a little bit further sexually. So far they have never gone all the way to intercourse. Keiko feels that the time she and Randy will have intercourse is close. Randy has agreed to wear a condom when they have intercourse, but he is embarrassed to get them himself. As a teenage girl, Keiko is also somewhat uncomfortable getting condoms. She is afraid she would be embarrassed to buy a package of condoms at the store, but she is not sure where else she might get condoms. In preparation to get them, she sits down to think of a less public place to get some condoms and to get her courage up to face the store clerks if she can think of nowhere else.

PEER EDUCATION

Teachers will find that peer education will be one of the most successful and useful ingredients they encounter in AIDS education. Peer education is exactly what it sounds like, students educating their peers. It is not a new concept, of course, and teachers might find its use practical in any number of subjects. Here we will discuss its application only to AIDS education.

As we have seen, the issues addressed in AIDS education tend to be very sensitive, and many instructors may be uneasy about confronting them directly. Peer education provides one method of getting around this problem. Students might be more comfortable receiving this information from other students of their own age. This is one way teachers can use peer pressure to work in a positive manner, as respected students teach others about AIDS prevention and the refusal skills by way of their words and deeds. Peer educators work as role models in the most basic definition of that term. Peer educators can also become invaluable assistants to teachers during the AIDS education unit. In addition to helping other students, peer educators also benefit from this experience. These students become empowered themselves by the program to protect themselves even more effectively against HIV and other STDs than they otherwise would have. This helps the peer educators raise their own self-esteem and feelings of empowerment, allowing them to take a much more active part in their own education than most students. They also strengthen their skills in presenting material and their confidence in speaking before groups. Just as we have seen with cooperative learning, peer education helps the peer educators understand the material more deeply by requiring them to explain it to others.

Because peer education makes demands on students' time and responsibility, it should be a voluntary assignment. Teachers might approach students who are respected by their peers in order to recruit them, but only those teens who demonstrate some interest and desire to become involved in peer education should be encouraged to join. Peer education can easily be undermined by a lack of attention. If the peer educators do not take their charge seriously, students who must learn from them will not take it seriously, either. Therefore, the best candidates to become peer educators would be those who already show themselves to be leaders among their peers. Honor students, student council officers, and athletes would be among the most obvious for teachers to enlist, but teachers should also not forget other types of leaders around them as well. Some students who do not strive to achieve scholastically or academically are respected by their peers as social leaders and maintain a strong influence over school styles and trends. In fact, this type of student might make a better peer educator than the "A" student who has little social contact with others. Teachers should keep in mind that their main concern is influencing behavior. Presenting facts and information is little more than a means to this end. In this same mode of thinking, teachers might seek to sign up recovering drug users or teen mothers as peer educators. Students who have had firsthand experience with risk behaviors and are willing to share the error of their ways can have a very profound influence on their peers, possibly serving as a personal warning of the costs of risky behavior. The broader a spectrum of the student body peer educators are able to represent, the greater the number of students they can reach and the wider their impact can be.

Training

Training the peer educators essentially involves a more intensive version of the program contained in this book. Because students training to be peer educators will be more enthusiastic about the program than most students in general, and because the size of the groups of peer educators is likely to be considerably smaller than normal class size, instructors will have an easier time training peer educators than they should expect with their regular classes. Teachers will be able to spend more time with and give more attention to each student, who in turn will be more eager to learn. Peer educators should learn the facts about HIV and AIDS, as well as become proficient in the refusal skills. While they should never be expected to replace their teachers in instructing their peers, peer educators should be able to function easily as teaching assistants. Beyond the program in general, peer educators should have some training in communication skills so they can more easily stand before their peers and other groups to present this information. If peer educators have mastered this material but are unable to convey it to their peers, their effectiveness will be virtually nil. Peer educators must be more than authorities in this subject, they must also be skilled communicators.

Depending on the response from administration, teachers may have to train peer educators after school in an extracurricular format. Some principals may be willing to let a class split itself in two, so some students can train to be peer educators while the rest of the class covers other material. Class time being at a premium, as it is in most schools, however, this solution may not be a practical one. If this is the case, teachers will be left with voluntary training sessions after school. The length of the sessions will depend upon student and teacher capabilities. Most programs will find ten to fifteen hours of training sufficient. A general health-related peer education program formed in a partnership between the Departments of Health and Education of Hawaii requires thirty hours of training, but this includes material on pregnancy, substance abuse, sexually transmitted diseases, and suicide in addition to HIV and AIDS.[1] Teachers desiring a broader-based peer education program might want to dedicate this amount of time to training, but teachers starting small and focusing primarily on HIV and AIDS can get away with a training program of shorter duration.

Determining the success of a peer education training program and the readiness of participants to educate their peers can be relatively easy. At the end of the training sessions, peer educators can prepare and deliver their own presentation on HIV and AIDS to the other peer educators. Depending upon how the teacher plans to utilize the peer educators, these presentations can go a number of ways. Some peer education programs require their participants to choose an area of specialty--perhaps HIV transmission, avoidance of risk situations, proper condom use, or something else. The peer educator should become a relative expert in this area, able to lead discussions and answer any questions on the topic that might be thrown at her or him. When facing topics outside this specialty area, the peer educator should be conversational but not necessarily expert. This approach lends itself to a team effort among the peer educators, in which they make joint presentations, with each team member focusing on his or her area of expertise. The end-of-training presentations would replicate what a peer educator would say to a class he or she was addressing. The other peer educators could ask questions, some easy, some more challenging, to test the speaker's knowledge and ability to present information to an audience.

Other peer education programs that might not have the resources to allow their peer educators to travel in groups prefer that their members have a wider but shallower pool of knowledge to draw from. These peer educators would be more likely to face a group on their own, without others to supplement their information. Their end-of-training presentations would all be quite similar to each other and would offer a more comprehensive overview of the AIDS issue. Once again, the other peer educators would be encouraged to play a tough audience, making the speaker work for their attention and challenging the speaker with questions. The teacher can use a pass-fail method of evaluation, determining what qualities an effective peer educator should have in this particular program. If a peer educator cannot successfully convey his or her material in a collegial environment such as this, he or she will have trouble addressing a classroom full of students who are unfamiliar with the subject. If a teacher intends to have peer educators do something other than make presentations, that teacher can determine his or her own test of readiness for peer educators. When peer educators can fulfill their function properly, they will be ready to enter the classroom.

Utilizing Peer Educators

Well-trained peer educators will prove their usefulness in a number of ways to teachers. Teenagers have an affinity for each other, and just the presence of other students among their instructors will make some students more open to learning about HIV and AIDS. Teachers who employ peer educators to convey facts and information on sensitive and controversial subjects find that their students respond more favorably to their peers than they do to adult authority figures.[2] In the minds of many students, their teachers "just don't get it." Peer educators at least come closer to "getting it." If possible, teachers might benefit from having some peer educators consult with them in planning and designing the AIDS education program. They can identify which aspects of the program are most likely to be successful. They might also have useful suggestions as to how students can best be reached with this information.

After teachers have initiated their program, they can bring in peer educators to help in the presentation. They can conduct their own miniclasses in AIDS education and offer special help to those students who seek it out. Some teachers have placed peer educators on a panel to field any questions that students might have. Students will often be more comfortable addressing questions to peers than to teachers, so peer educators have a better chance of confronting true student concerns than many teachers. Peer educators might also take the form of AIDS tutors, giving extra assistance to students who have trouble with the program. Instead of teachers modeling the skills enumerated in the previous chapter, peer educators can step in. They may have more credibility than teachers, as they could conceivably find themselves in quite similar situations in real life. At the very least, they could act as assistants to teachers whose refusal skills models require dialogue with another person. Peer educators can also write and perform skits that convey AIDS facts and portray the proper use of refusal skills. Beyond the informational aspects of peer education, these students can lead compelling discussions and present forceful arguments for teens maintaining responsible behavior or changing risky behavior. They can examine why students should strive to have responsible behavior, and how they might go about keeping or attaining it. When addressing a class or other group, peer educators might be confronted with questions to which they do not have the answer. In such situations, an honest response to that effect is best. Peer educators should never try to bluff a response about AIDS: the stakes are too high—if the peer educator provides misinformation, the cost could be someone's life. A lot of information on HIV and AIDS is easily accessible, and if someone is available to do a bit of research, an answer for most questions can be found before the end of a class or discussion session. Answers should be sought to all questions. If a class must return to a subject the next day in order to answer any leftover questions from the day before, that time should be allocated. If this occurs in a discussion group that is not meeting the next day, a peer educator should identify the student asking the question and provide the answer individually at a later time. If at all possible, peer educators should not leave any questions unanswered indefinitely.

Outside class, peer educators serve as role models, showing other students that risky behavior can be sidestepped without missing out on the various experiences of adolescence. Because of their position as peer educators, they may be approached by some students to offer counseling for general or particular problems. Because they have received training, they may be able to help other students remain abstinent or practice responsible sex. Peer educators have sometimes been found to have more success in intervening with at-risk students than have professional adult counselors.[3]

More ambitious peer education programs might reach beyond a single classroom to the entire school or even the community. Teachers might solicit their administration to consider making peer education an extracurricular service organization. Peer educators can effectively reach an entire student body through school assemblies in which they provide information and perform skits dramatizing the AIDS issue. On student service days, peer educators might staff their own display table to promote responsible sexual behavior. Schools that see quite a bit of success in a peer education program could "lend" their peer educators to other schools for single-class presentations or schoolwide assemblies. The initial motivation for training peer educators should be to help a class involved in an AIDS education program, but teachers should not think small. Peer education can extend beyond the subject of HIV and AIDS and beyond one classroom.

DRAMA

A relatively easy way to reach a large number of students is through the use of dramatic presentations. These can range from short black-outs and skits, to puppet shows, to full-length plays performed in a theatrical setting. The fourth wall of theater allows actors in character to address audiences on very personal subjects that might otherwise embarrass them offstage. A theatrical presentation also allows the audience to connect with ideas and characters without the entanglements or responsibilities that often complicate personal relationships. Audiences will allow themselves to be affected both emotionally and intellectually by this material. Once students are touched by the presentation and begin to identify with the characters who must face HIV infection, they will find their expectation of personal invulnerability challenged and slowly undermined. They may be unable to vocalize or even recognize such feelings, but their openness to the reality of HIV and AIDS will be heightened. If teachers combine dramatic presentations with group discussions, they will be able to introduce the subject of refusal skills and immediately follow up on any questions or misunderstandings.

AIDS education instructors may decide to use drama to provide a straightforward explanation of refusal skills, which would make these short plays very similar to the modeling techniques described in the previous chapter. Drama, however, can allow a broader range of choices than can modeling. Whereas modeling must demonstrate the correct methods of employing the skills, dramatic exhibitions can show how skills might be misused and the potential consequences of that misuse. Actors might portray teens who have become infected with HIV or, providing even more dramatic possibilities, a teen hospitalized with AIDS with his or her friends coming to visit. Very few people like hospitals, so the seriousness of the situation can quickly be made quite clear. Drama provides a much greater variety of possibilities than simple modeling, allowing performers to convey AIDS information, to promote responsible sexual behavior (including AIDS testing for those students who may be at risk), and to portray the realistic risk and consequences of HIV and AIDS that normal teens might face. Whenever possible, however, drama should not replace modeling, because skills modeling provides concise, specific information for avoiding risk situations. Dramatic presentations paint with a broader brush.

Teachers can utilize drama in several different aspects of AIDS education. They might employ dramatic means to present the facts and information vital to the understanding of the virus and its effects. In this instance, teachers might assign a dramatic presentation to a group of volunteers along with the other activities described in Chapter 5. Or peer educators may take it upon themselves to build a skit or even larger play into their arsenal of educational techniques. Instead of participating, students can watch peer educators enact different roles relating to HIV and AIDS. A third option might be to encourage some students to expand upon the role-plays described earlier. Instead of quick little scenarios following the style of the scenarios modeled by teachers, students might write a script for a more complicated situation that would involve a number of different characters. As suggested above, this script might follow a student who does not use the skills correctly and must face the consequences of risky behavior.

However teachers choose to employ dramatics in the classroom, skits or plays can be a very ambitious undertaking. Students will have an avenue through which to explore their creativity and an opportunity to make a more personal connection to the material than they would by simply sitting and listening to a lecture. Students might want to research the stories of various individuals who have had to confront HIV, either in their own lives or in the experience of friends and relatives. If students have trouble finding much information on any one person, they could easily write a series of vignettes incorporating the experiences of a number of people. These various people might be portrayed in scenes, featuring a number of performers, or in monologues, spotlighting only one performer at a time. A small group of actors might find it easier to focus on only one character for a monologue than to play a number of different parts in different ensemble pieces. Dramatic monologues also provide an outlet for students seeking extra credit. A student can write and perform a monologue alone, so a teacher who did not want to go to the trouble of organizing a full-fledged play can utilize drama in the classroom with a smaller effort.

Some students might be initially reluctant to participate in this type of dramatic production. If teachers find that a number of students resist becoming involved, they might fall back on using puppets rather than live actors. Puppet shows provide the performers with one more level of distance from the situation being portrayed. When puppets substitute for live actors, there is little to no chance that an audience would confuse a performer for the character he or she portrays. Puppets also provide the chance to remove racial, cultural, and sexual baggage that live performers can unintentionally bring with them. When presented with sensitive material such as this, audiences sometimes use any excuse to keep from identifying with the characters in a play. They might latch on to a character's ethnic identity to separate themselves, thinking that HIV only affects people like that character, not people like themselves. If various puppets are colored blue, green, yellow, purple, and orange, for instance, audiences do not have the opportunity to say, "AIDS is a disease of African Americans and homosexuals." Puppets by their very nature make the situation portrayed less threatening, allowing student audiences to become more receptive to the message.

Notes

Note to Preface

1. Paul Monette, *Borrowed Time: An AIDS Memoir* (San Diego: Harcourt Brace Jovanovich, 1988; New York: Avon Books, 1990): 18.

Notes to Chapter 1

1. Margaret L. Stuber, "Children, Adolescents and AIDS," *Psychiatric Medicine* 9 (1991): 441.

2. Marsha F. Goldsmith, "'Invisible' Epidemic Now Becoming Visible as HIV/AIDS Pandemic Reaches Adolescents," *Journal of the American Medical Association* 270 (July 7, 1993): 18.

3. Karen Hein, "'Getting Real' about HIV in Adolescents," *American Journal of Public Health* 83 (April 1993): 492.

4. Freya L. Sonenstein, Joseph H. Pleck, and Leighton C. Ku, "Sexual Activity, Condom Use and AIDS Awareness among Adolescent Males," *Family Planning Perspectives* 21 (July/August 1989): 153; Centers for Disease Control, "Premarital Sexual Experience among Adolescent Women—United States, 1970–1988," *Morbidity and Mortality Weekly Report* 39 (January 4, 1991): 930.

5. Virginia L. Tucker and Cheng T. Cho, "AIDS and Adolescents: How Can You Help Them Reduce Their Risk?" *AIDS and Adolescents* 89 (February 15, 1991): 49.

6. William L. Yarber and Anthony V. Parrillo, "Adolescents and Sexually Transmitted Diseases," *Journal of School Health* 62 (September 1992): 331.

7. Stuber, "Children, Adolescents and AIDS," pp. 444–445.

8. John E. Anderson, *et al.*, "HIV/AIDS Knowledge and Sexual Behavior among High School Students," *Family Planning Perspectives* 22 (November/December 1990): 254.

9. David Gelman, "The Young and the Restless," *Newsweek* (Jan 11, 1993): 60.

10. John S. Santelli and Peter Beilenson, "Risk Factors for Adolescent Sexual Behavior, Fertility, and Sexually Transmitted Diseases," *Journal of School Health* 62 (September 1992): 271, 273.

11. Jane E. Sisk, Maria Hewitt, and Kelly L. Metcalf, "The Effectiveness of AIDS Education," *Health Affairs* 7 (Winter 1988): 39.

12. Santelli and Beilenson, "Risk Factors," p. 273.

13. Karen Hein, "AIDS in Adolescence: Exploring the Challenge," *Journal of Adolescent Health Care* 10 (May 1989): 26S.

14. Rick Petosa and Janet Wessinger, "The AIDS Education Needs of Adolescents: A Theory-Based Approach," *AIDS Education and Prevention* 2 (1990): 134–135; Joan H. Skurnick, *et al*, "New Jersey High School Students' Knowledge, Attitudes, and Behavior Regarding AIDS," *AIDS Education and Prevention* 3 (1991): 29.

15. Santelli and Beilenson, "Risk Factors," p. 273.

16. Geri Loecker, *et al.*, "HIV Associated Risk Factors: A Survey of a Troubled Adolescent Population," *South Dakota Journal of Medicine* 45 (April 1992): 93.

17. Hein, "AIDS in Adolescence," pp. 14S–15S.

18. Raymond C. Bingham, "AIDS and Adolescents: Threat of Infection and Approaches for Prevention," *Journal of Early Adolescence* 9 (May 1989): 57.

19. Santelli and Beilenson, "Risk Factors," p. 277.

20. Stuber, "Children, Adolescents and AIDS," p. 450.

21. Yarber and Parrillo, "Adolescents and Sexually Transmitted Diseases," p. 333; Santelli and Beilenson, "Risk Factors," p. 275.

22. Santelli and Beilenson, "Risk Factors," p. 276.

23. Stacey B. Plichta, *et al.*, "Partner-Specific Condom Use among Adolescent Women Clients of a Family Planning Clinic," *Journal of Adolescent Health* 13 (September 1992): 509.

24. J. Holland, *et al.*, "Risk, Power and the Possibility of Pleasure: Young Women and Safer Sex," *AIDS Care* 4 (1992): 278.

25. Plichta, *et al.*, "Partner-Specific Condom Use," p. 510.

26. D. Wight, "Impediments to Safer Heterosexual Sex: A Review of Research with Young People," *AIDS Care* 4 (1992): 12–13.

27. R.S. Gold, *et al.*, "Situational Factors and Thought Processes Associated with Unprotected Intercourse in Heterosexual Students," *AIDS Care* 4 (1992): 320; Plichta, *et al.*, "Partner-Specific Condom Use," p. 510.

Notes to Chapter 2

1. Katherine E. Keough and George Seaton, "Superintendents' Views on AIDS: A National Survey," *Phi Delta Kappan* 69 (January 1988): 358–361.

2. Elizabeth G. Calamidas, "AIDS and STD Education: What's Really Happening in Our Schools?" *Journal of Sex Education and Therapy* 16 (1990): 61.

3. CDC, "Guidelines for School Health Education to Prevent the Spread of AIDS," *Morbidity and Mortality Weekly Report* 37 (Supplement 2) (January 29, 1988): 5.

4. John Leo, "Schools to Parents: Keep Out," *U.S. News & World Report* (October 5, 1992): 33; Donald R. Skillman and Charles Clark, "HIV Infection and the Acquired Immunodeficiency Syndrome: A Strategy for Public Education," *Military Medicine* 152 (September 1987): 480.

5. Carol K. Sigelman, *et al.*, "Parents' Contributions to Knowledge and Attitudes Regarding AIDS," *Journal of Pediatric Psychology* 18 (1993): 226–227.

6. Coalition of National Health Education Organizations, "Instruction about AIDS within the School Curriculum," *Journal of School Health* 58 (October 1988): 323.

7. Dan R. Denson, Robert Voight, and Russell Eisenman, "Factors that Influence HIV/AIDS Instruction in Schools," *Adolescence* 28 (Summer 1993): 312.

8. "Heterosexual AIDS: Pessimism, Pandemics, and Plain Hard Facts," *The Lancet* 341 (April 3, 1993): 364.

9. Calamidas, "AIDS and STD Education," p. 60.

10. Calamidas, "AIDS and STD Education," p. 59.

11. Vered Slonim-Nevo, Martha N. Ozawa, and Wendy F. Auslander, "Knowledge, Attitudes and Behaviors Related to AIDS among Youth in Residential Centers: Results from an Exploratory Study," *Journal of Adolescence* 14 (1991): 31–32.

12. W. James Popham, *et al*, "Evaluating the Effectiveness of a Re-

search-Based HIV Education Program," IOX Assessment Associates and Centers for Disease Control, 1993, photocopy: 20–21.

13. Calamidas, "AIDS and STD Education," p. 60.

14. Meg Gerrard, Monica Kurylo, and Theresa Reis, "Self-Esteem, Erotophobia, and Retention of Contraceptive and AIDS Information in the Classroom," *Journal of Applied Social Psychology* 21 (1991): 368–379.

15. Patricia L. Westerman and Philip M. Davidson, "Homophobic Attitudes and AIDS Risk Behavior of Adolescents," *Journal of Adolescent Health* 14 (1993): 208, 209.

16. Ralph Bolton, "AIDS and Promiscuity: Muddles in the Models of HIV Prevention," *Medical Anthropology* 14 (1992): 160.

Notes to Chapter 3

1. Simon Wain-Hobson, "Virological Mayhem," *Nature* 373 (January 12, 1995): 102.

2. "AIDS Numbers Increase under New Federal Rules," *New York Times*, March 22, 1993, sec. 2.

3. William A. Blattner, "HIV Epidemiology: Past, Present, and Future," *The FASEB Journal* 5 (July 1991): 2340.

4. Robyn M. Gershon, David Vlahov, and Kenrad E. Nelson, "HIV Infection Risk to Non Health-Care Workers," *American Industrial Hygiene Association Journal* 51 (December 1990): A-808.

5. Christopher J. Miller, Jerry R. McGhee, and Murray B. Gardner, "Mucosal Immunity, HIV Transmission, and AIDS," *Laboratory Investigation* 68 (February 1993): 138.

6. Miller, McGhee, and Gardner, "Mucosal Immunity," p. 139.

7. Marlene Cimons and Thomas H. Maugh II, "New Strategies Fuel Optimism in AIDS Fight," *Los Angeles Times*, February 20, 1995.

8. Gershon, Vlahov, and Nelson, "HIV Infection Risk," p. A-808.

9. "H.I.V. Clue Supports Early Use of Condom," *New York Times*, December 8, 1992, sec. 3.

10. "User Is Usually to Blame for Condom's Failure," *Los Angeles Times*, July 24, 1994, sec. 5.

11. Thomas R. Moench, *et al.*, "The Cat/Feline Immunodeficiency Virus Model for Transmucosal Transmission of AIDS: Nonoxynol-9 Contraceptive Jelly Blocks Transmission by an Infected Cell Inoculum," *AIDS* 7 (1993): 801.

12. Lee E. Klosinski, "Mother-to-Infant Transmission Patterns Better Understood," *Positive Living* 3 (March 1994): 8.

13. Herbert A. Perkins, "Safety of the Blood Supply," *Journal of Clinical Apheresis* 8 (1993): 114; Harold A. Kessler, *et al.*, "AIDS: Part I," *Disease-a-Month* 38 (September 1992): 664.

14. Gershon, Vlahov, and Nelson, "HIV Infection Risk," p. A-807.

15. Gershon, Vlahov, and Nelson, "HIV Infection Risk," p. A-808; Thomas C. Quinn, "The Epidemiology of the Human Immunodeficiency Virus," *Annals of Emergency Medicine* 19 (March 1990): 230.

16. Jose Esparza, "Why AIDS Cannot Be Transmitted by Insects," *International Nursing Review* 38 (September–October 1991): 137.

Notes to Chapter 4

1. Mary Lou Smith, Debbie Minden, and Arlette Lefevbre, "Knowledge and Attitudes about AIDS and AIDS Education in Elementary School Students and Their Parents," *Journal of School Psychology* 31 (1993): 287–288; Robert C. Goodhope, *et al.*, "What Teachers Think about AIDS," *South Dakota Journal of Medicine* 41 (May 1988): 32; Katherine E. Keough and George Seaton, "Superintendents' Views on AIDS: A National Survey," *Phi Delta Kappan* (January 1988): 361.

2. David F. Sly, *et al.*, "Young Children's Awareness, Knowledge, and Beliefs about AIDS: Observations from a Pretest," *AIDS Education and Prevention* 4 (1992): 231–232.

3. CDC, "Guidelines for Effective School Health Education to Prevent the Spread of AIDS," *Morbidity and Mortality Weekly Report* 37 (Supplement 2) (January 29,1988): 5.

4. Sly, *et al.*, "Young Children's Awareness," pp. 231–232.

5. CDC, "Guidelines for School Health Education," pp. 5–6.

6. CDC, "Guidelines for School Health Education," p. 6.

7. Susan L. Montauk and David M. Scoggin, "AIDS: Questions from Fifth and Sixth Grade Students," *Journal of School Health* 59 (September 1989): 291–295.

8. CDC, "Guidelines for School Health Education," p. 6.

9. CDC, "Guidelines for School Health Education," pp. 6–7.

10. CDC, "Guidelines for School Health Education," pp. 6–7.

11. CDC, "Guidelines for School Health Education," pp. 6–7.

12. CDC, "Guidelines for School Health Education," p. 7.

13. CDC, "Guidelines for School Health Education," p. 7.

14. CDC, "Guidelines for School Health Education," p. 7.

15. CDC, "Guidelines for School Health Education," p. 7.

16. CDC, "Guidelines for School Health Education," pp. 7–8.

Notes to Chapter 5

1. Kimberly Christensen, "Teaching Undergraduates about AIDS: An Action-Oriented Approach," *Harvard Educational Review* 61 (August 1991): 342–343.

2. A more detailed discussion of cooperative learning can be found in Robert E. Slavin, *Cooperative Learning* (New York: Longman, 1983).

3. Karen Hein, and the Editors of Consumer Reports Books, Theresa Foy DiGeronimo, *AIDS: Trading Facts for Fears* (Mount Vernon, NY: Consumers Union, 1989); Earvin "Magic" Johnson, *What You Can Do to Avoid AIDS* (New York: Times Books, 1992).

4. Steve M. Dorman, Parker A. Small, Jr., and Debra Dell Lee, "A Cooperative Learning Technique for AIDS Education," *Journal of School Health* 59 (September 1989): 314–315; Karen L. Bentrup, *et al.*, "Cooperative Learning: An Alternative for Adolescent AIDS Education," *The Clearing House* 64 (1990): 107–111.

Notes to Chapter 6

1. Jeanne T. Hernandez and Ralph J. DiClemente, "Self-Control and Ego Identity Development as Predictors of Unprotected Sex in Late Adolescent Males," *Journal of Adolescence* 15 (1992): 445.

2. Programs incorporating refusal skills against substance abuse are elucidated and evaluated in Arnold P. Goldstein, Kenneth W. Reagles, and Lester Amann, *Refusal Skills: Preventing Drug Use in Adolescents* (Champaign, IL: Research Press, 1990); Saladin K.T. Corbin, Russell T. Jones, and Robert S. Schulman, "Drug Refusal Behavior: The Relative Efficacy of Skills-Based and Information-Based Treatment," *Journal of Pediatric Psychiatry* 18 (1993): 769–784; Shewan Kim, Jonnie H. McLeod, and Carl Shantzis, "An Outcome Evaluation of Refusal Skills Program as a Drug Abuse Prevention Strategy," *Journal of Drug Education* 19 (1989): 363–371; Louise A. Rohrbach, *et al.*, "Evaluation of Resistance Skills Training Using Multitrait-Multimethod Role-Play Skill Assessments," *Health Education Research* 2 (1987): 401–407; Genice E. Turner, *et al.*, "Which Lesson Components Mediate Refusal Assertion Skill Improvement in School-Based Adolescent Tobacco Use Prevention?" *The International Journal of the Addictions* 28 (1993): 749–766.

Notes to Chapter 8

1. Edward Margulies and Kenneth Ito, "PEP: Peer Education in Health for Student Empowerment," *Hawaii Medical Journal* 49 (February 1990): 58.

2. Jennifer J. Shulkin, *et al.*, "Effects of a Peer-Led AIDS Intervention with University Students," *Journal of American College Health* 40 (September 1991): 76.

3. Myron L. Belfer, Penelope K. Krener, and Frank Black Miller, "AIDS in Children and Adolescents," *Journal of the American Academy of Child and Adolescent Psychiatry* 27 (1988): 148.

Bibliography

Abdool Karim, S.S., Abdool Karim, Q., Preston–Whyte, E., and Sankar
N. "Reasons for Lack of Condom Use among High School Students."
South Africa Medical Journal 82 (August 1992): 107–110.

"Adolescent Women—United States, 1970–1988." *Morbidity and Mortality Weekly Report* 39 (January 4, 1991): 930.

Aggleton, P. "When Will They Ever Learn? Young People, Health Promotion and HIV/AIDS Social Research." *AIDS Care* 3 (1991): 259–264.

"AIDS Attitude: Reacting to Persons with AIDS." *Journal of School Health* 63 (November 1993): 404–405.

"AIDS Community Demonstration Projects: Implementation of Volunteer Networks for HIV-Prevention Programs—Selected Sites, 1991–1992." *Morbidity and Mortality Weekly Report* 41 (November 20,1992): 868–869, 875–876.

"AIDS Prevention and Education." *Journal of Adolescent Health Care* 10 (1989): 45S–47S.

Allensworth, Diane DeMuth, and Symons, Cynthia Wolford. "A Theoretical Approach to School-Based HIV Prevention." *Journal of School Health* 59 (February 1989): 59–65.

Amer-Hirsch, Wendy. "Educating Youth about AIDS: A Model Program." *Children Today* 18 (September/October 1989): 16–19.

Anderson, John E., Kann, Laura, Holtzman, Deborah, Arday, Susan, Truman, Ben, and Kolbe, Lloyd. "HIV/AIDS Knowledge and Sexual Behavior among High School Students." *Family Planning Perspectives* 22 (November/December 1990): 252–255.

Archer, William, and Hein, Karen. "At Issue: Should AIDS-Prevention Programs for Teenagers Focus Exclusively on Sexual Abstinence?" *The CQ Researcher* 2 (December 25, 1992): 1137.

Arnold, Wendy. "PEP/LA Training Manual for Peer Educators." Peer Education Program of Los Angeles. Photocopy.

Atwood, Joan D. "A Multi-Systemic Approach to AIDS and Adolescents." *Child and Adolescent Social Work Journal* 9 (October 1992): 427–439.

Bandura, Albert. "Perceived Self-Efficacy in the Exercise of Control over AIDS Infection." *Evaluation and Program Planning* 13 (1990): 9–17.

Barron, James. "Learning the Facts of Life." *New York Times Educational Supplement* (November 8, 1987): 16–19.

Basch, Charles E. "Preventing AIDS through Education: Concepts, Strategies, and Research Priorities." *Journal of School Health* 59 (September 1989): 296–300.

Beck, Kenneth H. "The Health Education Video as Stone Soup." *Health Education Research* 5 (September 1990): 291–293.

Becker, Marshall H., and Joseph, Jill G. "AIDS and Behavioral Change to Reduce Risk: A Review." *American Journal of Public Health* 78 (April 1988): 392–410.

Belfer, Myron L., Krener, Penelope K., and Miller, Frank Black. "AIDS in Children and Adolescents." *Journal of the American Academy of Child Adolescent Psychiatry* 27 (1988): 147–151.

Bentrup, Karen L. Rienzo, Barbara A., Dorman, Steve M., and Lee, Debra Dell. "Cooperative Learning: An Alternative for Adolescent AIDS Education." *The Clearing House* 64 (November–December 1990): 107–111.

Berrenberg, Joy L., Rosnik, Daniel, and Kravcisin, Nicki J. "Blaming the Victim: When Disease-Prevention Programs Misfire." *Current Psychology: Research & Reviews* 9 (Winter 1990–1991): 415–420.

Biemiller, Lawrence. "Student-Health Experts Try Broad Approach in Combating AIDS." *The Chronicle of Higher Education* (September 2, 1992): A41–A43.

Bingham, Raymond C. "AIDS and Adolescents: Threat of Infection and

Approaches for Prevention." *Journal of Early Adolescence* 9 (May 1989): 50–66.

Black, Jeffrey Lynn, and Jones, Lorraine Henke. "HIV Infection: Educational Programs and Policies for School Personnel." *Journal of School Health* 58 (October 1988): 317–322.

Blake, Jeanne. *Risky Times: How to Be AIDS-Smart and Stay Healthy: A Guide for Teenagers.* New York: Workman Publishing, 1990.

Blattner, William A. "HIV Epidemiology: Past, Present, and Future," *The FASEB Journal* 5 (July 1991): 2340.

Bolton, Ralph. "AIDS and Promiscuity: Muddles in the Models of HIV Prevention." *Medical Anthropology* 14 (May 1992): 145–223.

Bolton, Ralph, and Singer, Merrill. "Introduction. Rethinking HIV Prevention: Critical Assessments of the Content and Delivery of AIDS Risk-Reduction Messages." *Medical Anthropology* 14 (May 1992): 139–143.

Breitman, Patti, Knutson, Kim, and Reed, Paul. *How to Persuade Your Lover to Use a Condom . . . and Why You Should.* Rocklin, CA: Prima Publishing and Communications, 1987.

Brown, Larry K., DiClemente, Ralph J., and Beausoleil, Nancy I. "Comparison of Human Immunodeficiency Virus Related Knowledge, Attitudes, Intentions, and Behaviors among Sexually Active and Abstinent Young Adolescents." *Journal of Adolescent Health* 13 (March 1992): 140–145.

Brown, Larry K., DiClemente, Ralph J., and Park, Teron. "Predictors of Condom Use in Sexually Active Adolescents." *Journal of Adolescent Health* 13 (December 1992): 651–657.

Brown, Larry K., and Fritz, Gregory K. "AIDS Education in the Schools: A Literature Review as a Guide for Curriculum Planning." *Clinical Pediatrics* 27 (July 1988): 311–316.

Brown, Larry K., Nassau, Jack H., and Barone, Vincent J. "Differences in AIDS Knowledge and Attitudes by Grade Level." *Journal of School Health* 60 (August 1990): 270–275.

Brown, Larry K., Nassau, Jack H., and Levy, Vivian. "'What Upsets Me Most about AIDS Is . . . ': A Survey of Children and Adolescents." *AIDS Education and Prevention* 2 (1990): 296–304.

Brown, William J. "An AIDS Prevention Campaign." *American Behavioral Scientist* 34 (July/August 1991): 666–678.

Calamidas, Elizabeth G. "AIDS and STD Education: What's Really Happening in Our Schools?" *Journal of Sex Education and Therapy* 16 (1990): 54–63.

_____. "Reaching Youth about AIDS: Challenges Confronting Health Educators." *Health Values* 15 (November/December 1991): 55–61.

Carlson, Michelle J. "Why Teens Need to Know about AIDS." *Ohio Medicine* 86 (May 1990): 366–368.

Centers for Disease Control, Center for Health Promotion and Education. "Guidelines for Effective School Health Education to Prevent the Spread of AIDS." *Morbidity and Mortality Weekly Report* 37, Supplement 2 (January 29, 1988): 1–14.

Centers for Disease Control, "Premarital Sexual Experience among Adolescent Women—United States, 1970-1988." *Morbidity and Mortality Weekly Report* 39, (January 4, 1991): 930.

Christensen, Kimberly. "Teaching Undergraduates about AIDS: An Action-Oriented Approach." *Harvard Educational Review* 61 (August 1991): 337–356.

Citizens Commission on AIDS for New York City and Northern New Jersey. "AIDS Prevention and Education: Reframing the Message." *AIDS Education and Prevention* 3 (1991): 147–163.

Coalition of National Health Education Organizations. "Instruction about AIDS within the School Curriculum." *Journal of School Health* 58 (October 1988): 323.

Collins, Janet L., and Britton, Patti O. *Training Educators in HIV Prevention: An Inservice Manual.* Santa Cruz, CA: Network Publications, a Division of ETR Associates, 1990.

Corbin, Saladin K.T., Jones, Russell T., and Schulman, Robert S. "Drug Refusal Behavior: The Relative Efficacy of Skills-Based and Information-Based Treatment." *Journal of Pediatric Psychology* 18 (1993): 769–784.

Dasen, Stephanie, Vaughan, Roger D., and Walter, Heather J. "Self-Efficacy for AIDS Preventive Behaviors among Tenth Grade Students." *Health Education Quarterly* 19 (Summer 1992): 187–202.

Davidson, Janis, and Grant, Chris. "Growing Up Is Hard to Do . . . in the AIDS Era." *MCN: American Journal of Maternal Child Nursing* 13 (September–October 1988): 352–356.

De Loye, Gerald J., Henggeler, Scott W., and Daniels, Christine M. "Developmental and Family Correlates of Children's Knowledge and Attitudes Regarding AIDS." *Journal of Pediatric Psychology* 18 (1993): 209–219.

Denson, Dan R., Voight, Robert, and Eisenman, Russell. "Factors that Influence HIV/AIDS Instruction in Schools." *Adolescence* 28 (Summer 1993): 309–314.

Diamant, Anita. "Kids and AIDS: What You *Must* Tell Your Children." *Parents* (March 1993): 74–77.

DiClemente, Ralph J. "Epidemiology of AIDS, HIV Prevalence, and HIV

Incidence among Adolescents." *Journal of School Health* 62 (September 1992): 325–330.

_____. "Preventing HIV/AIDS among Adolescents: Schools as Agents of Behavior Change." *Journal of the American Medical Association* 270 (August 11, 1993): 760–762.

_____, ed. *Adolescents and AIDS: A Generation in Jeopardy.* Newbury Park, CA: Sage Publications, 1992.

DiClemente, Ralph J., Boyer, Cherrie B., and Mills, Stephen J. "Prevention of AIDS among Adolescents: Strategies for the Development of Comprehensive Risk-Reduction Health Education Programs." *Health Education Research* 2 (1987): 287–291.

DiClemente, Ralph J., Brown, Larry K., Beausoleil, Nancy I., and Lodico, Mark. "Comparison of AIDS Knowledge and HIV-Related Sexual Risk Behaviors among Adolescents in Low and High AIDS Prevalence Communities." *Journal of Adolescent Health* 14 (May 1993): 231–236.

Dorman, Steve M., Small, Parker A., Jr., and Lee, Debra Dell. "A Cooperative Learning Technique for AIDS Education." *Journal of School Health* 59 (September 1989): 314–315.

DuRant, Robert H., Ashworth, Carolyn Seymore, Newman, Cheryl, and Gaillard, Greg. "High School Students' Knowledge of HIV/AIDS and Perceived Risk of Currently Having AIDS." *Journal of School Health* 62 (February 1992): 59–63.

DuRant, Robert H., Ashworth, Carolyn Seymore, Newman, Cheryl, McGill, Cindy Rabun, and Baranowski, Tom. "AIDS/HIV Knowledge Level and Perceived Chance of Having HIV among Rural Adolescents." *Journal of Adolescent Health* 13 (September 1992): 499–505.

Edgar, Timothy, Freimuth, Vicki S., and Hammond, Sharon L. "Communicating the AIDS Risk to College Students: The Problem of Motivating Change." *Health Education Research* 3 (1988): 59–65.

Ennew, Judith. "Preventive Intervention Programmes in Adolescence: Education in Safe Sexual Behaviour for Life?" *Crisis* 10 (1989): 78–87.

Esparza, Jose. "Why AIDS Cannot Be Transmitted by Insects." *International Nursing Review* 38 (September–October 1991): 137.

Farrell, Larry D., and Girvan, James T. "AIDS Education—An Opportunity for Interdisciplinary Networking." *Education* 110 (Spring 1990): 352–355.

Fennell, Reginald, and Beyrer, Mary K. "AIDS: Some Ethical Considerations for the Health Educator." *Journal of American College Health* 38 (November 1989): 145–147.

Fisher, Jeffrey D., and Fisher, William A. "Changing AIDS-Risk Behavior." *Psychological Bulletin* 111 (1992): 455–474.

Flora, June A., and Thoresen, Carl E. "Reducing the Risk of AIDS in Adolescents." *American Psychologist* 43 (November 1988): 965–970.

Ford, Kathleen, and Norris, Anne E. "Knowledge of AIDS Transmission, Risk Behavior, and Perceptions of Risk among Urban, Low-Income, African-American and Hispanic Youth." *American Journal of Preventive Medicine* 9 (1993): 297–306.

_____. "Urban African-American and Hispanic Adolescents and Young Adults: Who Do They Talk to about AIDS and Condoms? What Are They Learning?" *AIDS Education and Prevention* 3 (1991): 197–206.

Forrest, Jacqueline Darroch, and Silverman, Jane. "What Public School Teachers Teach about Preventing Pregnancy, AIDS and Sexually Transmitted Diseases." *Family Planning Perspectives* 21 (March/April 1989): 65–72.

France, Kim. "AIDS Explodes among Teens." *Utne Reader* (July/August 1992): 30, 32.

Franzini, Louis R., Sideman, Lawrence M., Dexter, Klarisse E., and Elder, John P. "Promoting Aids Risk Reduction via Behavioral Training." *AIDS Education and Prevention* 2 (1990): 313–321.

Freudenberg, Nicholas. *Preventing AIDS: A Guide to Effective Education for the Prevention of HIV Infection*. Washington, DC: American Public Health Association, 1989.

Froner, Geoffrey, and Rowniak, Stefan. "The Health Outreach Team: Taking AIDS Education and Health Care to the Streets." *AIDS Education and Prevention* 1 (1989): 105–118.

Futrell, Mary H. "AIDS Education through Schools." *Journal of School Health* 58 (October 1988): 324–326.

Gabriel, V., and Packham, D.R. "Heterosexual Transmission: A Growing Risk Factor for HIV Spread." *Australia and New Zealand Journal of Obstetrics and Gynaecology* 33 (1993): 174–176.

Gardner, William, and Herman, Janna. "Adolescents' AIDS Risk Taking: A Rational Choice Perspective." In *Adolescents in the AIDS Epidemic*, edited by William Gardner, Susan G. Millstein, and Brian L. Wilcox, *New Directions for Child Development* 50 (Winter 1990): 17–34.

Gellin, Bruce G., and Rogers, David E. "The Stalled Response to AIDS." *Issues in Science and Technology* 9 (Fall 1992): 24–28.

Gelman, David. "The Young and the Reckless." *Newsweek* (January 11, 1993): 60–61.

Gerrard, Meg, Kurylo, Monica, and Reis, Theresa. "Self-Esteem, Erotophobia, and Retention of Contraceptive and AIDS Information in the Classroom." *Journal of Applied Social Psychology* 21 (1991): 368–379.

Gershon, Robyn M., Vlahov, David, and Nelson, Kenrad E. "HIV Infection Risk to Non Health-Care Workers." *American Industrial Hygiene Association Journal* 51 (December 1990): A808.

Getzel, George S., and Mahony, Kevin. "Education for Life during the AIDS Pandemic." *Social Casework: The Journal of Contemporary Social Work* (June 1988): 396–399.

Gibbs, Nancy. "How Should We Teach Our Children about Sex?" *Time* (May 24, 1993): 60–66.

_____. "Teens: The Rising Risk of AIDS." *Time* (September 2, 1991): 60–61.

Gilliam, Aisha, Scott, Marcia, and Troup, Jean. "AIDS Education and Risk Reduction for Homeless Women and Children: Implications for Health Education." *Health Education* 20 (December 1989): 44–47.

Gold, R.S., Karmiloff-Smith, A., Skinner, M.J., and Morton, J. "Situational Factors and Thought Processes Associated with Unprotected Intercourse in Heterosexual Students." *AIDS Care* 4 (1992): 305–323.

Goldsmith, Marsha F. "'Invisible' Epidemic Now Becoming Visible as HIV/AIDS Pandemic Reaches Adolescents." *Journal of the American Medical Association* 270 (July 7, 1993): 16, 18–19.

Goldstein, Arnold P., Reagles, Kenneth W., and Amann, Lester. *Refusal Skills: Preventing Drug Use in Adolescents.* Champaign, IL: Research Press, 1990.

Goodhope, Robert C., Ball, Gerald C., Koenig, Laura L., Mollerud, Christine L., Oakland, Lars E., and Leonardson, Gary R. "What Teachers Think about AIDS." *South Dakota Journal of Medicine* 41 (May 1988): 29–35.

Greig, Russell, and Raphael, Beverley. "AIDS Prevention and Adolescents." *Community Health Studies* 13 (1989): 211–219.

Hacker, Sylvia S. "AIDS Education Is Sex Education: Rural and Urban Challenges." *Journal of Social Work and Human Sexuality* 8 (1989): 155–170.

Halleron, Trish, Pisaneschi, Janet, and Trapani, Margi, eds. *Learning AIDS: An Information Resources Directory.* 2d ed. New York: R.R. Bowker: 1989.

Haven, Grant G., and Stolz, Jeffrey W. "Students Teaching AIDS to Students: Addressing AIDS in the Adolescent Population." *Public Health Reports* 104 (January–February): 75–79.

Hein, Karen. "AIDS in Adolescence: Exploring the Challenge." *Journal of Adolescent Health Care* 10 (May 1989): 10S–35S.

_____. "Commentary on Adolescent Acquired Immunodeficiency Syndrome: The Next Wave of the Human Immunodeficiency Virus Epidemic?" *The Journal of Pediatrics* 114 (January 1989): 144–149.

_____. "Fighting AIDS in Adolescents." *Issues in Science and Technology* 7 (Spring 1991): 67–72.

_____. "'Getting Real' about HIV in Adolescents." *American Journal of Public Health* 83 (April 1993): 492–494.

Hein, Karen, DiGeronimo, Theresa Foy, and the Editors of Consumer Reports Books. *AIDS: Trading Fears for Facts.* Mount Vernon, NY: Consumers Union, 1989.

Helgerson, Steven D., Peterson, Lyle R., and the AIDS Education Study Group. "Acquired Immunodeficiency Syndrome and Secondary School Students: Their Knowledge Is Limited and They Want to Learn More." *Pediatrics* 81 (March 1988): 350–355.

Henggeler, Scott W., Melton, Gary B., and Rodrigue, James R. *Pediatric and Adolescent AIDS: Research Findings from the Social Sciences.* Newbury Park, CA: Sage Publications, 1992.

Hernandez, Jeanne T., and DiClemente, Ralph J. "Self-Control and Ego Identity Development as Predictors of Unprotected Sex in Late Adolescent Males." *Journal of Adolescence* 15 (1992): 437–447.

Herold, Edward S., Fisher, William A., Smith, Edward A., and Yarber, William A. "Sex Education and the Prevention of STD/AIDS and Pregnancy among Youths." *Canadian Journal of Public Health* 81 (March/April 1990): 141–145.

"Heterosexual AIDS: Pessimism, Pandemics, and Plain Hard Facts." *The Lancet* 341 (April 3, 1993): 863–864.

Hingson, Ralph, Strunin, Lee, and Berlin, Beth. "Acquired Immunodeficiency Syndrome Transmission: Changes in Knowledge and Behaviors among Teenagers, Massachusetts Statewide Surveys, 1986 to 1988." *Pediatrics* 85 (January 1990): 24–29.

"HIV Instruction and Selected HIV-Risk Behaviors among High School Students—United States, 1989–1991." *Morbidity and Mortality Weekly Report* 41 (November 20, 1992): 866–868.

Hochhauser, Mark, and Rothenberger, James H. *AIDS Education.* Dubuque, IA: Wm. C. Brown Publishers, 1992.

Holland, J., Ramazanoglu, C., Scott, S., Sharpe, S., and Thomson, R. "Risk, Power and the Possibility of Pleasure: Young Women and Safer Sex." *AIDS Care* 4 (1992): 273–283.

House, Reese M., and Walker, Catherine M. "Preventing AIDS via Education." *Journal of Counseling and Development* 71 (January/February 1993): 282–289.

Howard, Marion, and McCabe, Judith Blamey. "Helping Teenagers Postpone Sexual Involvement." *Family Planning Perspectives* 22 (January/February 1990): 21–26.

Ikpa, Vivian W. "Schools Must Effectively Educate Students, Staff and Faculty and Community Members Regarding AIDS Epidemic." *Education* 112: 459–463.

Jemmott, John B., Jemmott, Loretta Sweet, Spears, Hazel, Hewitt, Nicole, and Cruz-Collins, Madeline. "Self-Efficacy, Hedonistic Expectancies, and Condom-Use Intentions among Inner-City Black Adolescent Women: A Social Cognitive Approach to AIDS Risk Behavior." *Journal of Adolescent Health* 13 (September 1992): 512–519.

Johnson, Earvin "Magic." *What You Can Do to Avoid AIDS.* New York: Times Books (Random House), 1992.

Jones, Russell T., McDonald, Daniel W., Fiore, Michael F., Arrington, Thadeus, and Randall, Jeff. "A Primary Preventive Approach to Children's Drug Refusal Behavior: The Impact of Rehearsal-Plus." *Journal of Pediatric Psychology* 15 (1990): 211–223.

Kaplan, Barbara J., and Shayne, Vivian T. "Unsafe Sex: Decision-Making Biases and Heuristics." *Aids Education and Prevention* 5 (1993): 294–301.

Katz, Roger C., Robisch, Christine M., and Telch, Michael J. "Acquisition of Smoking Refusal Skills in Junior High School Students." *Addictive Behaviors* 14 (1989): 201–204.

Keeling, Richard P. "HIV Disease: Current Concepts." *Journal of Counseling and Development* 71 (January/February 1993): 261–274.

Kelley, Barbara Bailey. "Education Needed as Incidence of AIDS Rises among Teens." *Utne Reader* (July/August 1990): 94 (Excerpted from Pacific News Service, February 2, 1990).

Kelly, Jeffrey A., and Murphy, D.A. "Some Lessons Learned about Risk Reduction after Ten Years of the HIV/AIDS Epidemic." *AIDS Care* 3 (1991): 251–257.

Kelly, Jeffrey A., St. Lawrence, Janet S., Betts, Ron, Brasfield, Ted L., and Hood, Harold V. "A Skills-Training Group Intervention Model to Assist Persons in Reducing Risk Behaviors for HIV Infection." *AIDS Education and Prevention* 2 (1990): 24–35.

Kelly, Jeffrey A., St. Lawrence, Janet S., Hood, Harold V., and Brasfield, Ted L. "Behavioral Intervention to Reduce AIDS Risk Activities." *Journal of Consulting and Clinical Psychology* 57 (1989): 60–67.

Keough, Katherine E., and Seaton, George. "Superintendents' Views on AIDS: A National Survey." *Phi Delta Kappan* (January 1988): 358–361.

Kerr, Dianne L. "Students Need Skills to Prevent HIV Infection." *Journal of School Health* 60 (January 1990): 39.

Kessler, Harold A., *et al.* "AIDS: Part I." *Disease–a–Month* 38 (September 1992): 664.

Kim, Sehwan, McLeod, Jonnie H., and Shantzis, Carl. "An Outcome Evaluation of Refusal Skills Program as a Drug Abuse Prevention Strategy." *Journal of Drug Education* 19 (1989): 363–371.

Kirby, Douglas. "School-Based Programs to Reduce Sexual Risk-Taking Behaviors." *Journal of School Health* 62 (September 1992): 280–287.

Klosinski, Lee E. "Mother-to-Infant Transmission Patterns Better Understood." *Positive Living* 3 (March 1994): 8.

Koblinsky, Sally A., and Preston, Janet E. "Why We *Must* Teach about AIDS." *Vocational Education Journal* 64 (September 1989): 20, 22.

Kok, Gerjo. "Health Education Theories and Research for AIDS Prevention." *Hygie* 10 (1991–1992): 32–39.

Kolbe, Lloyd, Jones, Jack, Nelson, Gary, Daily, Lisa, Duncan, Carlton, Kann, Laura, Lawrence, Andrea, Broyles, Beth, and Poehler, David. "School Health Education to Prevent the Spread of AIDS: Overview of a National Programme." *Hygie* 7 (1988): 10–13.

Koop, C. Everett. "From the Surgeon General, U.S. Public Health Service." Introduction to "Surgeon General's Report on Acquired Immune Deficiency Syndrome." *Journal of the American Medical Association* 256 (November 28, 1986): 2783.

Kraft, Joe W., Bostic, Jeff Q., and Tallent, Mary K. "West Texas Teenagers and AIDS: A Survey of Their Knowledge, Attitudes, Behavioral Changes, and Information Sources." *Texas Medicine* 86 (September 1990): 74–78.

Ku, Leighton C., Sonenstein, Freya L., and Pleck, Joseph H. "The Association of AIDS Education and Sex Education with Sexual Behavior and Condom Use among Teenage Men." *Family Planning Perspectives* 24 (May–June 1992): 100–106.

Laver, M.L. Susan. "AIDS Education Is More than Telling People What Not to Do." *Tropical Doctor* 23 (October 1993): 156–160.

Lawrence, Lyn, Levy, Susan R., and Rubinson, Laurna. "Self-Efficacy and AIDS Prevention for Pregnant Teens." *Journal of School Health* 60 (January 1990): 19–24.

Leo, John. "Schools to Parents: Keep One." *U.S. News & World Report,* (October 5, 1992): 33.

Leslie-Harwit, M., and Meheus, A. "Sexually Transmitted Disease in Young People: The Importance of Health Education." *Sexually Transmitted Diseases* (January–March 1989): 15–20.

Leviton, Laura C., and Valdiserri, Ronald O. "Evaluating AIDS Prevention: Outcome, Implementation, and Mediating Variables." *Evaluation and Program Planning* 13 (1990): 55–66.

Levy, Susan R., Lampman, Claudia, Handler, Arden, Flay, Brian R., and Weeks, Kyle. "Young Adolescent Attitudes toward Sex and Substance Use: Implications for AIDS Prevention." *AIDS Education and Prevention* 5 (1993): 340–351.

Loecker, Geri, Smith, David A., Smith, Leah, and Bunger, Patricia. "HIV Associated Risk Factors: A Survey of a Troubled Adolescent Population." *South Dakota Journal of Medicine* 45 (April 1992): 91–94.

Longshore, Douglas. "AIDS Education for Three High-Risk Populations." *Evaluation and Program Planning* 13 (1990): 67–72.

Los Angeles Times. January 1987–February 1995.

Madaras, Lynda. *Lynda Madaras Talks to Teens about AIDS: An Essential Guide for Parents, Teachers, and Young People.* New York: Newmarket Press, 1988.

Majer, Lani Smith, Santelli, John S., and Coyle, Karin. "Adolescent Reproductive Health: Roles for School Personnel in Prevention and Early Intervention." *Journal of School Health* 62 (September 1992): 294–297.

Manning, D. Thompson, and Balson, Paul M. "Teenagers' Beliefs about AIDS Education and Physicians' Perceptions about Them." *The Journal of Family Practice* 29 (1989): 173–177.

Margulies, Edward, and Ito, Kenneth. "PEP: Peer Education in Health for Student Empowerment." *Hawaii Medical Journal* 49 (February 1990): 57–59.

Marsa, Linda. "Teaching AIDS." *Omni* (April 1990): 18–20.

McNulty, Charles. "AIDS Education through Theater: NYU's Creative Arts Team." *Theater* 23 (Spring 1992): 41–43.

Meisenbach, Bert. "Is Value-Free Sex Talk Valuable?" *Journal of American College Health* 40 (September 1991): 99–100.

Mellanby, Alex, Philips, Fran, and Tripp, John. "Sex Education: More Is Not Enough." *Journal of Adolescence* 15 (1992): 449–466.

Miller, Christopher J., McGhee, Jerry R., and Gardener, Murray B. "Mucosal Immunity, HIV Transmission, and AIDS," *Laboratory Investigation* 68 (February 1993): 138.

Miller, Leslie, and Downer, Ann. "AIDS: What You and Your Friends Need to Know—A Lesson Plan for Adolescents." *Journal of School Health* 58 (April 1988): 137–141.

Moench, Thomas R., *et al.* "The Cat/Feline Immunodeficiency Virus Model for Transmucosal Transmission of AIDS: Nonoxynol-9 Contraceptive Jelly Blocks Transmission by an Infected Cell Inoculum," *AIDS* 7 (1993): 801.

Monette, Paul. *Borrowed Time: An AIDS Memoir,* San Diego: Harcourt Brace Jovanovich, 1988; New York: Avon Books, 1990.

Montauk, Susan L., and Scoggin, David M. "AIDS: Questions from Fifth and Sixth Grade Students." *Journal of School Health* 59 (September 1989): 291–295.

Moore, Susan M., and Rosenthal, Doreen A. "Condoms and Coitus: Adolescents [*sic*] Attitudes to AIDS and Safe Sex Behavior." *Journal of Adolescence* 14 (1991): 211–227.

———. "The Social Context of Adolescent Sexuality: Safe Sex Implications." *Journal of Adolescence* 15 (1992): 415–435.

Moskal, Rosemary J. "Effect of a Comprehensive AIDS Curriculum on Knowledge and Attitudinal Changes in Northern Canadian College Students." *Canadian Journal of Counselling* 25 (1991): 338–349.

New York Times. January 1987–February 1995.

Newcomer, Susan, and Baldwin, Wendy. "Demographics of Adolescent Sexual Behavior, Contraception, Pregnancy, and STDs." *Journal of School Health* 62 (September 1992): 265–270.

Obeidallah, Dawn, Turner, Patricia, Iannotti, Ronald J., O'Brien, Robert W., Haynie, Denise, and Galper, Daniel. "Investigating Children's Knowledge and Understanding of AIDS." *Journal of School Health* 63 (March 1993): 125–129.

Osborne, Mary L., Kistner, Janet A., and Helgemo, Benjamin. "Developmental Progression in Children's Knowledge of AIDS: Implications for Education and Attitudinal Change." *Journal of Pediatric Psychology* 18 (1993): 177–192.

Ostrow, David G. "AIDS Prevention through Effective Education." *Daedalus* 118 (Summer 1989): 229–254.

Pendergrast, Robert A., Jr., DuRant, Robert H., and Gaillard, Gregory L. "Attitudinal and Behavioral Correlates of Condom Use in Urban Adolescent Males." *Journal of Adolescent Health* 13 (March 1992): 133–139.

Perkins, Herbert A. "Safety of the Blood Supply." *Journal of Clinical Apheresis* 8 (1993): 114.

Perry, Cheryl L. "Prevention of Alcohol Use and Abuse in Adolescence: Teacher- vs. Peer-Led Intervention." *Crisis* 10 (1989): 52–61.

Petosa, Rick, and Jackson, Kirby. "Using the Health Belief Model to Predict Safer Sex Intentions among Adolescents." *Health Education Quarterly* 18 (Winter 1991): 463–476.

Petosa, Rick, and Wessinger, Janet. "The AIDS Education Needs of Adolescents: A Theory-Based Approach." *AIDS Education and Prevention* 2 (1990): 127–136.

Plichta, Stacey B., Weisman, Carol S., Nathanson, Constance A., Ensminger, Margaret E., and Robinson, J. Courtland. "Partner-Specific Condom Use among Adolescent Women Clients of a Family Planning Clinic." *Journal of Adolescent Health* 13 (September 1992): 506–511.

Pollack, Amy E. "Teen Contraception in the 1990s." *Journal of School Health* 62 (September 1992): 288–293.

Popham, W. James, Hall, Elizabeth H., Muthén, Linda K., King, Susan M., Banspach, Stephen W., Collins, Janet L., and Rugg, Deborah L. "Evaluating the Effectiveness of a Research-Based HIV Education Program." IOX Assessment Associates and the Centers for Disease Control, 1993. Photocopy.

Post, Stephen G. "Adolescents in a Time of AIDS: Preventive Education." *America* (17 October 1992): 278–282.

"Program: AIDS Peer Education Exchange." *Health Education Quarterly* 19 (Winter 1992): 425.

Quackenbush, Marcia, and Nelson, Mary, with Clark, Kay, eds. *The AIDS Challenge: Prevention Education for Young People.* Santa Cruz, CA: Network Publications, a Division of ETR Associates, 1988.

Quackenbush, Marcia, and Sargent, Pamela. *Teaching AIDS: A Resource Guide on Acquired Immune Deficiency Syndrome.* Santa Cruz, CA: Network Publications, a Division of ETR Associates, 1988.

Quackenbush, Marcia, and Villarreal, Sylvia. *"Does AIDS Hurt?" Educating Young Children about AIDS.* Santa Cruz, CA: Network Publications, a Division of ETR Associates, 1988.

Quinn, Thomas C. "The Epidemiology of the Human Immunodeficiency Virus." *Annals of Emergency Medicine* 19 (March 1990): 230

Quirk, Mark E., Godkin, Michael A., and Schwenzfeier, Elizabeth. "Evaluation of Two AIDS Prevention Interventions for Inner-City Adolescent and Young Adult Women." *American Journal of Preventive Medicine* 9 (1993): 21–26.

Remafedi, Gary. "The Impact of Training on School Professionals' Knowledge, Beliefs, and Behaviors Regarding HIV/AIDS and Adolescent Homosexuality." *Journal of School Health* 63 (March 1993): 153–157.

Rohrbach, Louise A., Graham, John W., Hansen, William B., Flay, Brian R., and Johnson, C. Anderson. "Evaluation of Resistance Skills Training Using Multitrait-Multimethod Role-Play Skill Assessments." *Health Education Research* 2 (1987): 401–407.

Romer, D., and Hornik, R. "HIV Education for Youth: the Importance of Social Consensus in Behaviour Change." *AIDS Care* 4 (1992): 285–303.

Rosenberger, Judith, and Wineburgh, Marsha. "Working with Denial: A Critical Aspect in AIDS Risk Intervention." *Social Work in Health Care* 17 (1992): 11–26.

Ross, Michael W., and Rosser, B.R. Simon. "Education and AIDS Risks: A Review." *Health Education Research* 4 (1989): 273–284.

Rotheram-Borus, Mary Jane, Becker, Judith V., Koopman, Cheryl, and Kaplan, Meg. "AIDS Knowledge and Beliefs, and Sexual Behavior of Sexually Delinquent and Non-Delinquent (Runaway) Adolescents." *Journal of Adolescence* 14 (1991): 229–244.

Rotheram-Borus, Mary Jane, and Koopman, Cheryl. "HIV and Adolescents." *The Journal of Primary Prevention* 12 (1991): 65–82.

Rotheram-Borus, Mary Jane, Koopman, Cheryl, Haignere, Clara, and Davies, Mark. "Reducing HIV Sexual Risk Behaviors among Runaway Adolescents." *Journal of the American Medical Association* 266 (September 4, 1991): 1237–1241.

Sabatier, Renee C. "AIDS Education: Evolving Approaches." *Canadian Journal of Public Health* 80 (May/June 1989): S9–S11.

Santelli, John S., and Beilenson, Peter. "Risk Factors for Adolescent Sexual Behavior, Fertility, and Sexually Transmitted Diseases." *Journal of School Health* 62 (September 1992): 271–279.

Santelli, John S., and Kirby, Douglas. "Adolescent Sexuality: Pregnancy, Sexually Transmitted Disease, and Prevention." *Journal of School Health* 62 (September 1992): 262–264.

Sawyer, Robin G., and Beck, Kenneth H. "Effects of Videotapes on Perceived Susceptibility to HIV/AIDS among University Freshmen." *Health Values* 15 (March/April 1991): 31–40.

Schaalma, Herman P., Peters, Louk, and Kok, Gerjo. "Reactions among Dutch Youth toward People with AIDS." *Journal of School Health* 63 (April 1993): 182–187.

Schonfeld, David J., Johnson, Susan R., Perrin, Ellen C., O'Hare, Linda L., and Cicchetti, Domenic V. "Understanding of Acquired Immunodeficiency Syndrome by Elementary School Children—A Developmental Survey." *Pediatrics* 92 (September 1993): 389–395.

Shulkin, Jennifer J., Mayer, Joni A., Wessel, Leland G., de Moor, Carl, Elder, John P., and Franzini, Louis R. "Effects of a Peer-Led AIDS Intervention with University Students." *Journal of American College Health* 40 (September 1991): 75–79.

Siegel, David, Lazarus, Nancy, Krasnovsky, Flora, Durbin, Meg, and Chesney, Margaret. "AIDS Knowledge, Attitudes, and Behavior among Inner City Junior High School Students." *Journal of School Health* 61 (April 1991): 160–165.

Sigelman, Carol K., Derenowski, Eileen B., Mullaney, Helene A., and Siders, Annice T. "Parents' Contributions to Knowledge and Attitudes Regarding AIDS." *Journal of Pediatric Psychology* 18 (1993): 221–235.

Silin, Jonathan G. "Children, Teachers, and the Human Immunodeficiency Virus: Authorizing AIDS Education in the Curriculum." *Journal of Education* 174 (November 1, 1992): 52–69.

Sims, John C.R. "Proposals for Improving AIDS Education in South Carolina." *The Journal of the South Carolina Medical Association* 88 (December 1992): 577–580.

Sisk, Jane E., Hewitt, Maria, and Metcalf, Kelly L. "The Effectiveness of AIDS Education." *Health Affairs* 7 (Winter 1988): 37–51.

Skillman, Donald R., and Clark, Charles. "HIV Infection and the Acquired Immunodeficiency Syndrome: A Strategy for Public Education." *Military Medicine* 152 (September 1987): 479–480.

Skinner, D., Metcalf, C.A., Seager, J.R., de Swarde, J.S., and Laubscher, J.A. "An Evaluation of an Education Programme on HIV Infection Using Puppetry and Street Theatre." *AIDS Care* 3 (1991): 317–329.

Skurnick, Joan H., Johnson, Robert L., Quinones, Mark A., Foster, James D., and Louria, Donald B. "New Jersey High School Students' Knowledge, Attitudes, and Behavior Regarding AIDS." *AIDS Education and Prevention* 3 (1991): 21–30.

Slavin, Robert E. *Cooperative Learning.* New York: Longman, 1983.

Slonim-Nevo, Vered, Ozawa, Martha N., and Auslander, Wendy F. "Knowledge, Attitudes and Behaviors Related to AIDS among Youth in Residential Centers: Results from an Exploratory Study." *Journal of Adolescence* 14 (1991): 17–33.

Sly, David F., Eberstein, Isaac W., Quadagno, David, and Kistner, Janet A. "Young Children's Awareness, Knowledge, and Beliefs about AIDS: Observations from a Pretest." *AIDS Education and Prevention* 4 (1992): 227–239.

Smith, Edward A., and Dickson, Lenore L. "The Impact of a Condom Desensitization Program on Female College Students." *Health Values* 17 (May/June 1993): 21–31.

Smith, Mary Lou, Minden, Debbie, and Lefebvre, Arlette. "Knowledge and Attitudes about AIDS and AIDS Education in Elementary School Students and Their Parents." *Journal of School Psychology* 31 (1993): 281–292.

Solomon, Mildred Zeldes, and DeJong, William. "Recent Sexually Transmitted Disease Prevention Efforts and Their Implications for

AIDS Health Education." *Health Education Quarterly* 13 (Winter 1986): 301–316.

Sonenstein, Freya L., Pleck, Joseph H., and Ku, Leighton C. "Sexual Activity, Condom Use and AIDS Awareness among Adolescent Males." *Family Planning Perspectives* 21 (July/August 1989): 152–158.

Sorenson, Robert E. *Adolescent Sexuality in Contemporary America.* New York: World Publishing, 1973.

Speece, Susan P. "AIDS Education in the Science Classroom." *The American Biology Teacher* 54 (January 1992): 13–15.

Stewart, Susan A. and Beazley, Richard P. "Meeting a Person with AIDS in the Classroom: An Evaluation." *Canadian Journal of Public Health* 84 (July/August 1993): 265–268.

Stuber, Margeret L. "Children, Adolescents and AIDS." *Psychiatric Medicine* 9 (1991): 441–454.

"Students Teach AIDS to Students." *The Futurist* (September–October 1990): 52–53.

Taylor, Clark L., and Lourea, David. "HIV Prevention: A Dramaturgical Analysis and Practical Guide to Creating Safer Sex Interventions." *Medical Anthropology* 14 (1992): 243–284.

"Teen AIDS Education Found Lacking." *Facts on File* 52 (April 16, 1992): 273–274.

Ting, David, and Carter, James H. "Behavioral Change through Empowerment: Prevention of AIDS." *Journal of the National Medical Association* 84 (1990): 225–228.

Tolsma, Dennis D. "Activities of the Centers for Disease Control in AIDS Education." *Journal of School Health* 58 (April 1988): 133–136.

Tonks, Douglas. "Can You Save Your Students' Lives? Educating to Prevent AIDS." *Educational Leadership* 50 (December 1992/January 1993): 48–51.

Tucker, Virgina L., and Cho, Cheng T. "AIDS and Adolescents: How Can You Help Them Reduce Their Risk?" *AIDS and Adolescents* 89 (February 15, 1991): 49–53.

Turner, Genice E., Burciaga, Catherine, Sussman, Steve, Klein-Selski, Eva, Craig, Sande, Dent, Clyde W., Mason, Hyacinth R.C., Burton, Dee, and Flay, Brian. "Which Lesson Components Mediate Refusal Assertion Skill Improvement in School-Based Adolescent Tobacco Use Prevention?" *The International Journal of the Addictions* 28 (1993): 749–766.

Valdiserri, Ronald O. *Preventing AIDS: The Design of Effective Programs.* New York: Rutgers University Press, 1989.

Valentich, Mary, and Gripton, James. "Teaching Children about AIDS." *Journal of Sex Education and Therapy* 15 (1989): 92–102.

Vicenzi, Angela E., and Thiel, Robert. "AIDS Education on the College Campus: Roy's Adaptation Model Directs Inquiry." *Public Health Nursing* 9 (December 1992): 270–276.

Wain-Hobson, Simon. "Virology Mayhem." *Nature* 373 (January 12, 1995): 102.

Walsh, Mary E., and Bibace, Roger. "Children's Conceptions of AIDS: A Developmental Analysis." *Journal of Pediatric Psychology* 16 (1991): 273–285.

Walter, Heather J., and Vaughan, Roger D. "AIDS Risk Reduction among a Multiethnic Sample of Urban High School Students." *Journal of the American Medical Association* 270 (August 11, 1993): 725–730.

Ward, Laurien. "Drama: An Effective Way to Educate about AIDS." *Social Casework: The Journal of Contemporary Social Work* 69 (June 1988): 393–396.

Weinman, Maxine L., Smith, Peggy B., and Mumford, David M. "A Comparison Between a 1986 and 1989 Cohort of Inner-City Adolescent Females on Knowledge, Beliefs, and Risk Factors for AIDS." *Journal of Adolescence* 15 (1992): 19–28.

Wenger, Neil S., Greenberg, Jerome N., Hilbornt, Lee H., Kusseling, Francoise, Mangotich, Maureen, and Shapiro, Martin F. "Effect of HIV Antibody Testing and AIDS Education on Communication about HIV Risk and Sexual Behavior." *Annals of Internal Medicine* 117 (December 1, 1992): 905–911.

Westerman, Patricia L., and Davidson, Philip M. "Homophobic Attitudes and AIDS Risk Behavior of Adolescents." *Journal of Adolescent Health* (1993): 208–213.

White, David M., and Matthews, Sue M. "AIDS and the Immune System." *Journal of School Health* 58 (October 1988): 339–340.

White, Hazel L. "What Teachers Should Know about AIDS." *The Clearing House* 64 (May/June 1991): 343–345.

Wight, Daniel. "Impediments to Safer Heterosexual Sex: A Review of Research with Young People." *AIDS Care* 4 (1992): 11–21.

———. "A Re-Assessment of Health Education on HIV/AIDS for Young Heterosexuals." *Health Education Research* 8 (1993): 473–483.

Wilce, Hilary. "In Virgin Territory." *Times Educational Supplement* (October 16, 1992): section 2.

Williams, Richard, and Ponton, Lynn. "HIV and Adolescents: An International Perspective." *Journal of Adolescence* 15 (1992): 335–343.

Wyatt, H.V. "Ambiguities and Scares in Educational Material about AIDS." *AIDS Education and Prevention* 1 (1989): 119–125.

Yam, Philip. "AIDS Education May Breed Intolerance." *Scientific American* (September 1991): 30.

Yarber, William L. "What Makes a Good AIDS Curriculum?" *The Education Digest* (May 1988): 49–51. (Condensed from *PTA Today* 13, February 1988, 8–10.)

Yarber, William L., and Parrillo, Anthony V. "Adolescents and Sexually Transmitted Diseases." *Journal of School Health* 62 (September 1992): 331–338.

Zimet, Gregory D., Hillier, Sherry A., Anglin, Trina M., and Ellick, Elise M. "Knowing Someone with AIDS: The Impact on Adolescents." *Journal of Pediatric Psychology* 16 (1991): 287–294.

Index